CONCILIUM

CONCILIUM
ADVISORY COMMITTEE

CONCILIUM 2009/4

MONOTHEISM – DIVINITY AND UNITY RECONSIDERED

Edited by

Erik Borgman, Maria Clara Bingemer, and
Andrés Torres Queiruga

SCM Press · London

Published by SCM Press, 13–17 Long Lane, London EC1A 9PN

Copyright © International Association of Conciliar Theology, Madras (India)

www.concilium.in

English translations copyright © 2009 SCM-Canterbury Press Ltd

ISBN 978 0 334 03105 5

Printed in the UK by
CPI William Clowes, Beccles NR34 7TL

Concilium published March, June, August, October,
December

Contents

Part Three: Theological Forum

Editorial

'You shall have no other gods before me' (Deut. 5.7): The Oneness of God in a Plural World

A few decades ago it seemed very obvious to anyone living in the West that monotheism was the only possible religious option. This is coherent with what the biblical traditions – Judaic and Christian – and the Koran assert and maintain: that the oneness of God is also a matter of revelation, and therefore of faith. Since the Enlightenment and particularly the great modern and idealist philosophers have questioned the whole world-view that had prevailed till then, the question of the oneness of God has also begun to surface once more. According to some sectors in society and in the Church, belief in a single God came to be not just a truth of faith but also – and equally – an intuition of pure reason. Nevertheless, the plurality of the contemporary world, the fragmentation of the apparently solid structure of modernity, produced an equally plural view of the world. And this had an impact on religion as much as on other dimensions of human life.

As a result, in the most recent critiques made of the Enlightenment with the coming of so-called post-modernity, unity is particularly under attack. Situated at the centre of modern thought, unity is accused of being responsible for establishing and confirming the logic of hierarchical order and exclusion of difference. And this profits those who are in the centres of power and who define and decide how the world is and above all how it should be. At the same time, they exclude those who are on the margins of the modern process and progress from access to alternatives. Their outlook often appears derivative, obsolete, and mistaken, their beliefs superstitious or magical. They are made 'other' in relation to the central Western model. They are at best tolerated as exotic, at worst culturally annihilated and even physically destroyed.

After the events of 11 September 2001, other important questions were raised: was monotheistic faith generating fanaticisms and fundamentalisms that, in their turn, are engendering violence throughout the planet? Could the monotheistic faiths be a source of exclusion and, as a result, of violence and intolerance? Furthermore: could the God the so-called monotheistic faiths adore and proclaim be so exclusive and destructive by nature?

According to many critiques, yes, he is. The God of Judaism, of Christianity, of Islam is not just violent in practice, as he clearly appears to be from many passages in the Holy Books of these religions, but the quest for uniqueness and their constant endeavours to exclude plurality and ambivalence from their view of the world, expressed in their adherence to a one and only God, leaves these religions open to accusations of being violent on principle. The Enlightenment saw monotheism as the intellectually highest form of religious understanding because of its conviction that the Absolute had to be one and only. According to Enlightenment logic and critique, on the other hand, polytheism could be seen as ethically better because it would escape from the obsession with unity and hierarchy and favour and even stimulate plurality. These discussions and their backdrop are presented in the introductory article in this issue of *Concilium*.

In the book of Deuteronomy, the oneness of God is given as an aspect of the power and liberative character of the One God: 'I am the Lord your God, who brought you out of Egypt, out of the house of slavery; you shall have no other gods before me' (Deut. 5.6–7). The people of God are commanded to avoid adoring any other divinities beside the liberator God. What is being excluded here is not plurality but the possibility of thinking of oppressive powers as truly divine. The liberator God is God from before the Creation to the end of history, by when all the powers will be shown once and for all to be non-existent and powerless.

In other words, there are more than enough reasons for re-investigating theologically what we understand by and what is the meaning of 'oneness' and 'plurality' in religious traditions. Speaking of them in terms of 'monotheism' and 'polytheism' can be deceptive. So the first three articles in the first part of this issue analyze the framework of oneness in relation to diversity in different religions. The final one in this section presents a critique of the concepts of 'monotheism' and 'polytheism' in the history of study of religions.

Nevertheless, even if one can show that the unity and uniqueness of God in the monotheistic traditions is not the exclusive oneness attacked by the Enlightenment, it remains true that monotheistic faith has often been at the centre of conflict and disputes over the past centuries. And it is equally true that it still is today. For those who inherit the biblical traditions, the very commandment not to have other gods before the true God who liberates, understood within a certain mindset, could give the impression of excluding any other form of belief.

The second part of this issue identifies and develops alternative ways of understanding and practising God's unity within Christian traditions. This part concludes with a view of the oneness and uniqueness of God that is liberating without excluding, and of the faith of the community of believers in this God as specific without forming a static and excluding identity.

Finally, the 'Theological Forum' follows the theme of monotheism with Rosino Gibellini's examination of Jan Assmann's controversial *Moses the Egyptian* and assesses other personalities and events with contemporary relevance: the legacy of Karl Rahner twenty-five years after his death; the Christian humanism of Simone Weil; and the impact made by (former bishop) President Lugo of Paraguay.

The Editors would like to thank the following for their help in preparing this issue: Puy Ruiz de Larramedi, Fritz P. Schaller, Marie-Theres Wacker, Diego Irarrazabal, Rosino Gibellini, Felix Wilfred.

Translated by Paul Burns

Introduction

Philosophical, Political, and Ethical Problems of Unity and Plurality, Monotheism and Polytheism

PIERRE GIBERT S.J.

'I am secretly attracted to polytheism. . . . The fact is, intellectually at least, I find polytheism more satisfying or, in other words, monotheism gives rise to as many difficulties as it resolves, if ever it does that anyway . . .'

Hervé Tremblay O.P.

I.

In a recent study of the origins of biblical monotheism in a theological journal, a Dominican exegete and theologian made the above unashamed admission at the beginning of part two of an article on 'Yahweh or Baal?'. He continued thus: 'The truth is, if there is only one eternal and omnipotent God, we have to describe how he relates to the world; we have to justify evil in all its forms; and we have to explain why what happens in the world so rarely accords with his well-meaning plans. Intellectually, we are much more inclined to accept good gods in constant conflict with bad gods than one God overall. . . .'[1]

We are certainly unaccustomed to reading this kind of 'confession' and, what is more, one couched in such rationalistic language, from not merely a Christian writer but an exegete and theologian. In the present context, since the last decades of the previous century in fact, we have learned to expect another, quite novel and radical, approach, which consists of citing the dangerous, indeed perverse, nature of monotheism. There is also an implicit reference to polytheism, the traditional opposite and opponent of monotheism, whose 'more human' plurality is now deemed to be advantageous. From this viewpoint, the acceptance of polytheism would involve condemning the singularity of monotheism because of its supposed self- sufficiency and the violence to which it gives rise, especially because of a 'law' which the one God would be inclined to impose in the manner of a dictator or a totalitarian system. Accordingly, in obedience to a kind of new humanism, we would have to discard the accumulated evidence that had caused the relegation to the garbage dump of human history of all forms of polytheism, which human reason had invalidated definitively anyway.

Indeed, in the West at least, we thought we had finished with polytheism ages ago, although its surviving traces still to be found in other cultures and religions aroused the interest, even if with a certain condescension at times, of all ethnographers and historians of religion. These scholars could then lay claim to a sympathetic (even scholarly or scientific) curiosity, over against the excessively committed, far too interested attitude of missionaries and a more or less unconsciously self-congratulatory enthusiasm for an exclusive monotheism. In fact, even if it no longer seems to be self-evident, even if that were demanded by all forms of atheism, monotheism would still have to be opposed from a cultural, indeed anthropological viewpoint, because of the implications of the primarily intellectual, then historical, and even existential violence involved in asserting its 'uniqueness'. The foregoing is something like the present context of the questions posed by monotheism versus polytheism, irrespective of the validity of some or all of these issues.

It seems appropriate to ask whether this new inquiry (which is not devoid of a certain polemical tone) might not also conceal some surprisingly positive elements as far as new data and therefore new grounds for reflection are concerned.

What exactly do we mean when we use the term 'monotheism'? Is its contrary really as 'absurd' as it seems? Are we so sure of the exactitude of our terminology and its implications when speaking along these lines, especially when we refer to the 'three great monotheistic religions', as if the differences between them were somehow rendered insignificant by so fundamental an acknowledgement of their status?

II.

In the very first place, we must not forget or overlook the fact that monotheism is derived from polytheism to some extent, whatever might be said of a kind of basic monotheism that is more or less explicit, sometimes assumed to present in the background of any polytheistic cult, and, as befits the nature of a higher divinity, absolutely transcendent, and the source of everything, including the multiple divinities of polytheism. The latter are honoured because they are accessible and especially because of a certain dangerous quality not attributed to any kind of unattainable divinity consequently devoid of risk or interest. Worshippers the course of whose everyday lives made them more directly vulnerable begged the favours of the various deities interested in or aroused by their problems; of, that is, the celebrated gods and goddesses of earth and sky, moon or stars, trees and springs, and so forth, who of course were all located below the divine order that people sensed but had no need to worry about.

At the same time, in practice, the acknowledgement of a kind of elective and devotional monotheism in the personal choice of a divinity to which one was devoted individually, as a family, or as a civic function, could also serve to relativize a polytheism whose more or less genealogical lack of definition would have rendered almost impracticable otherwise, yet without arriving at the level of the monotheism as imposed by the corpus of the Bible at the height of its doctrinal supremacy.

In particular, however, in order to establish an exclusive divine uniqueness as against all that, our own terminologies have in fact adopted from the sphere of polytheism certain generic designations derived from the personal names of individual deities. The Latin *Deus*, like its almost homonymic Greek synonym, *Theos*, is particularly reminiscent of Zeus; and similarly the generic *El* is inevitably reminiscent of the chthonic deity to which it was formerly attached, and *a fortiori* of its plural *Elohim* (in the singular in Israel, of course), and consequently of the Arab *Allah*, from the same Semitic root. Even *Yhwh*, the ultimate Uniqueness in accordance with the biblical acceptation of the name, is now recognized as having previously designated a god in the pantheon of Canaan, one that is even said to have been a minor divinity.

In other words, any designation of the sole god (or only God) making an historical appearance in association with a particular polytheism would retain, between the lines as it were, a certain semantic trace of its former association and, correlatively, a certain degree of doctrinal ambiguity. Of course we should remember that the one God of Israel, irreversibly removed from a one-time polytheism both condemned and in principle forgotten, did not avoid the intermediate stage of monolatry, or that of the one god of a nation able to permit the acknowledgement of other divinities in other nations, or even within one and the same nation.

III.

From the viewpoint of the history of religions, neither monotheism nor polytheism can be so easily dismissed, when we recall the complexity of the circumstances constantly cited by historians or even philosophers of religion. Perhaps the recent questioning of monotheism in conjunction with a more or less approbative reference to polytheism is merely the latest moment in a series of vicissitudes, and these did not actually conclude with a Christianity and Islam already considerably indebted to a Judaism that had freed itself with difficulty from its particular form of polytheism.

In fact this was the outcome of a slow, complex process of development that eventually had to accept that monotheism was indisputable. This was attributable to the triumph of a reason prepared by certain philosophers since the Greece of classical antiquity. Here we need only refer to the first few chapters of the *Summa* of St Thomas Aquinas in order to avoid any additional historical investigation, especially in the West, where all forms of (more or less anti-Christian) deism and theism were compelled to justify themselves by appealing to evidence established by rational argument.

What has happened in recent decades to call in question this association of incontrovertibility and understanding between monotheism and reason, sometimes so very emphatically or affirmatively as to brook no contradiction? Need we do no more than cite the spirit of the age and particular circumstances that challenged a necessarily exclusive monotheism more insistently than ever before, without necessarily calling for a return to some form of polytheism, and wished to eradicate all forms of monotheism as instruments of an evil and dangerous ideology?

In my opinion, and within the scope of my knowledge, two sets of tendencies have supported this line of argument: either those based on examples drawn from the past history and even more from the present practice of a specific monotheistic religion, or those arising from a personal rejection of family pressure and of a religious tradition that commentators would accuse of nullifying all recourse to others, and all respect for them. In the first case, the intention would be to adduce the traditional citation of the Inquisition in the Western Church, then that of recent manifestations of 'Islamism', in order to justify the castigation of a 'murderous' monotheism; in the second case, an attack based on personal experience would claim to detect the operation of a 'violent' form of alienation in religion: one that seeks to impose its principles and laws on individual consciences through the totalitarianism of a single god, without recourse to any alternative.

It would probably be easy to disprove the validity of such aggressive, over-emotional and polemical accusations, quite apart from their confusion in general and in detail, since proponents of monotheism could easily cite indisputable evidence of its acceptability. But in the present context this approach might well fail if two or three aspects of monotheism, or polytheism, were to invite a different way of seeing things, preventing straightforward recourse and reversion to what had been accepted as obvious for so long.

IV.

A certain number of recent adverse critiques encourage the questioning of what had seemed to be established for thousands of years, first by philosophy and later by theology, before being definitively crowned by biblical 'revelation'. Might we say that between the castigation of the 'pernicious effects' of the monotheistic religions, those infamous sources of murderous violence, and the implied intellectually reductive limitation of the basic concept of unity and uniqueness, monotheism is doomed to incur the sentence of definitive unjustifiability, even though that does not mean that polytheism stands on any safer ground, given the present instances of a globalization that disallows any kind of compartmentalization and any indifference to or lack of awareness of reality? Monotheism would surely then have come under the influence of a rational position, and accordingly would be held to have moved more or less relatively, if not improperly, beyond a former stage of awareness and of thought?

At this stage, 'religion' would be understood primarily as an institution of collective adherence, without any explicit expression of any notion of belief whatsoever, and naturally far removed from rational thought. Moral and ritual practices would also depend on a consensus within which practice and behaviour would also be just as relative. But, on the other hand, surely it would be much easier to oppose the alternative to this rejection of monotheism, since it is difficult to attribute positive qualities to polytheism in general in all its forms, and to recognize them across the board, because that would necessarily mean including instances of atheism that have been legitimized at a state level? But since the crimes of some never justify the crimes of others, the question posed now is one of the validity and legitimacy of the affirmation of monotheism, from either an historical or a rational point of view. But here we have to inquire into the actual – existential – import of these categories.

V.

Monotheism and polytheism are primarily abstractions that rely on general-ization and do not precisely designate or objectify anything very much. I have alluded to the possible superficial or false aspects of each term with regard to the 'three great monotheistic religions'. Apart from a few vague points in common and a common mythic source ('We are all sons of Abraham'), surely there are rather more differences and contrasts between them than any puta-tive essential fundamental agreement?

An examination of theological conceptions in this regard reveals different components, including opposition to this notion of a common 'monothe-ism', to the point where Islam views Christianity as an idolatrous religion, that is, ultimately a polytheistic religion, while Judaism cannot accept the fact that Jesus of Nazareth should be so emphatically held to be the 'Son of God', and not merely treated as messiah in name, as with the *Shema Israel* of Deuteronomy. On the other hand, studies currently under way of the origins of Islam and their relations to Judeo-Christian (or anti-trinitarian and therefore heretical) Christian communities, refer to data that are com-plex in another way, and not necessarily devoid of polytheistic manifestations which Muhammad would have been compelled to oppose.

To return to the source more or less recognized or accepted by these 'three monotheisms', the Old Testament insists in this regard on data that invite us to ask whether the categories invoked here are too straightforward or simple. In other words, to investigate a possible source may enable us to establish not only the facts and conditions governing the emergence of a specific phenomenon, which would be that of monotheism in the present instance, but of what that phenomenon allowed to be deployed throughout the making of a corpus which remained complex all the way to its culmination in the New Testament.

Of course the uniqueness of God that establishes the definitive bases of monotheism is to be found in Deuteronomy and Exodus, and especially in the first part of the Decalogue, and there is no lack of texts that run counter to any abstraction from this uniqueness. I shall not digress on the subject of poetic expressions which, particularly in the psalms, appear to incorporate 'elohim' (in this connection I am thinking especially of creative Wisdom as presented in Proverbs chapter 8, especially Prov. 8.22–31). Even though the Prophets are absolutely punctilious defenders of the worship and recogni-tion of the one Yhwh, their apocalyptic heritage features figures involved in the world of 'shades' in which the one God is not reduced to solitariness.

In parallel with these data of the sapiential or apocalyptic type, which are above suspicion as far as any idolatrous derivation is concerned, we also have to take account of criticism directed against figures and representations.

Certainly a critique of idols appears in the Old Testament redactions, and certainly there are all but fundamental instances of opposition to 'images' whose aesthetics would still be tempting for more or less convinced 'iconoclasts'. But there is just as much criticism and certainly relativization of the figures and images under whose guise God decides to appear. We need only recall the 'critique' of theophanies when Yahweh reveals himself to Elijah on Horeb, the mountain of God, not in the earthquake or the wind or the lightning but in a gentle whisper.

But perhaps it is a culminating point of the canon of scripture that is more important here: the fact that all the divine manifestations and representations in the Old Testament culminate in the New Testament at the end of the Prologue to John's Gospel, at the point of the assertion that 'No one has ever seen God'. In other words, the God of strict monotheism has always eluded human vision! But the effect of this affirmation, which disallows numerous illusions, is to introduce the manifestation of divine fullness in the Son, that is, in Christ, which means in the One who will be described ultimately as the second Person of the Holy Trinity. At this point, in effect, it is appropriate to ask whether ultimately the existing acceptations and supposed antagonism between polytheism and monotheism are not instances of convenient wordplay that define no aspect whatsoever of what they are supposed to designate? What reality would they actually refer to? If polytheism has been entirely emptied of relevance by monotheism, surely the latter would be rendered just as completely void in its turn by the very complexity of the essential thrust of biblical revelation? Who is God? Is he to be found in his uniqueness? But no one has ever seen him, other than the One who has emerged from closest intimacy with the Father.

Islam might well view this as a reversion to polytheism, and Judaism as an erroneous understanding of God as person. But surely Christianity should refuse to get involved in an argument about the strict designations of monotheism just as much as one about those of polytheism? What if it was a matter of false designations as well as false distinctions? It is more important to scrutinize these classifications now than ever before, but just as much by reason of that dynamic biblical thrust which, throughout the Old Testament, but especially at its culminating point in the New Testament, would force us to shift the emphases, or even merely to decide that these two terms are inappropriate, because they are not exact designations of the gods of polytheism or of the one God of monotheism. Reflection on the Trinity would be more necessary than ever to 'de-abstractize' and thereby disclose the divine order enclosed in these terms and their contrarieties.

Translated by J.G. Cumming

Note

1. Hervé Tremblay, O.P., 'Yahvé contre Baal? Ou plutôt Yahvé à la place de Baal? Jalons pour la naissance d'un monothéisme. II. Le conflit entre Canaan/Baal et Israël/Yahvé selon les textes', *Science et Esprit. Revue de Théologie et de Philosophie*, Vol. 61(2009), January–April issue, fasc. 1, p. 51.

Part One: Dealing with Plurality and Unity in Religious Traditions

Biblical Monotheism between Dispute and Re-vision. Christian and Old Testament Viewpoints

MARIE-THERES WACKER

For something like thirty years, Old Testament scholars have conducted a debate about biblical monotheism, its origins, and its consequences. Of course the topic as such is far from new. The concept of an 'ethical and prophetic monotheism' was deployed in the mid-nineteenth century in an attempt to conceive of belief in God in ancient Israel as a process of development from an ethnically to an ethically informed religion, and to embed it in the overall perspective of a rationally inspired religious evolution. But the present-day hermeneutical context is novel in many respects, as are the images that result from a reconstruction of the history of religion in Israel and from a redefinition of central biblical texts and traditions. Moreover, as I seek to demonstrate in the following pages, Old Testament scholarship is not only directed by the immanent rationale proper to research, but reacts characteristically to contemporary questioning of biblically grounded monotheism as a future religious and theological option.

I. Multiform development

Whereas the notion of 'ethical monotheism' was a product of liberal Protestant exegesis in western Europe, new lines of thought have appeared in the discussion of monotheism since the 1980s. Within Catholicism, the second Vatican Council released biblical scholarship from the confines of neo-scholastic determinism and allowed it access, first and foremost, to the methods and formulations of Protestant historico-critical exegesis. Catholic exegetes have provided some of the most creative contributions to the recent exegetical treatment of monotheism.[1] Not only western European and North American Christian commentators, but Jewish biblical scholars from North

America and archaeologists from Israel have also taken up the subject over
the last few years.[2] Moreover, differently nuanced contributions from feminist or gender-sensitive perspectives have added new views to the gender-
neutral scholarly mainstream.[3]

A common feature of these new voices is that they lead to a critical revi-
sion not only of the presumptions of religious historical research in the past
regarding religious history and history in general, but of reactions to those
presumptions on the part of biblical and salvation history. New paradigms
have come into play in the meantime, such as, in particular, a concept of a
form of 'settlement' that would require early Israel to be viewed not as a
group of people that had made their way into this area from outside, but as
an 'indigenous people' that had made the transition from a semi-nomadic to
a settled way of life.[4] Then the origins of Israel would lie in the land itself,
and the religion of Israel could not be understood as having been in total
contrast to the religion of 'Canaan' but as simultaneously continuous and
discontinuous with it.

The new paradigms are associated with the further development and
delineation of methods of historico-exegetical research. In this respect, special mention should be made of the form of iconography that systematically
elicits the significance of the countless seals and amulets, statuettes and other
image-bearing artefacts from the area of ancient Israel, and discloses their
value for the reconstruction of a history of religion that is not dependent
on the scriptural texts.[5] At the same time, new forms of literary-critical and
literary-historical exegesis have developed; these allocate a central position
to the biblical text and its structures and concentrate on a highly-nuanced
analysis of the relationship between the text itself, the historical contexts in
which it originated, and the specific contexts of its reception. An important
consequence of this has been a new boost to dating the literature of the Old
Testament. Contrary to the tendency to ascribe greater age to theologically
significant biblical traditions, as advocated by traditional form criticism, there
has been an increasing trend to attribute relevant phenomena to more recent
eras in the history of Israel. In particular, the Decalogue is now considered
to be a subsequent compendium of contentious items from a long way into
the Israelite kingship period, and is no longer held to be a normative text
derived from a period as far back as the pre-State epoch. In research into the
Prophets and prophetism, the onetime assurance that it is possible to reason
a posteriori from the prophetic books to the great individual prophetic figures
of the eighth to sixth centuries B.C., and their impulse to achieve a religious
reformation in pre-exilic Israel, is now treated with cautious scepticism. The

dominant aspect of the prophetic writings seems to be the elaborate overall composition, behind which the historical profile of the individual prophetic personality would now appear to be ascertainable only with difficulty.

The variations within the discipline referred to in the foregoing impinge on new theological presuppositions. Christian theology after the Holocaust has become more sensitive to its own anti-Semitic prejudices, even in the supposedly 'objective' constructions of the history of Israel. Therefore Christian Old Testament scholars exhibit greater wariness in dealing with the common monotheistic heritage. Then there is Christian openness to a dialogue with world religions, especially with Judaism and Islam as closely-related monotheistic religions. On the other hand, contextual theologies of the kind possible throughout the world introduce the specific problems, but also the specific symbolic resources, of particular regions to theology. At the same time, they draw attention to the historical constants of Western colonialism with its multiple economic, ecological, social, and cultural effects, which also prevail in the purviews of the Christian Churches. Biblical monotheism is included in these critical revisions, and its concentration on divine uniqueness is suspected of excluding all variety and multifarious features. We are most emphatically alerted to the fact that the language of force as met with in many – in fact, far too many – scriptural texts is 'semantic dynamite',[6] a dangerous potential that could lead to the repeated promotion of religiously motivated violence in the name of the one God.

How are the origin and outlines of biblical monotheism to be described and interpreted against this background?

II. Soteriological monolatry and 'feudal loyalty'

The traditional translation of the so-called First Commandment of the Decalogue (Exod. 20.3 / Deut. 5.7) is: 'You shall have no other gods before me'. The Book of Exodus is concerned with the people of Israel that made its way out of Egypt and is now assembled at the foot of Mount Sinai. As we follow the course of the narrative from this point back into the books of Exodus and Genesis, it is evident that the biblical narrator sees the God who reveals himself on Sinai as none other than the God who created heaven and earth (Gen. 1).

Nevertheless, the formulation of the First Commandment cannot be understood appropriately in either religious-historical or theological terms if it is conceived of as expressing biblical 'monotheism', thereby invoking a concept with a traditional theological acceptation specified by the doctrine of the existence of the one, unique, personal God who transcends this world. The First Commandment does not in fact assert the existence only of one God, but requires the worship only of Yahweh, as is explicitly stated a few verses later on (Exod. 20.5 / Deut. 5.9). Therefore it does not formulate any kind of philosophical interpretation, but calls for practical action. It does not controvert polytheism, but presupposes it and restricts it only within Israel.[7] Consequently, as far as the history of religion is concerned, the demand made by the First Commandment may be described more appropriately as a demand for Yahweh-monolatry – for the worship of Yahweh alone in Israel. The reconstructions of recent exegetical monotheism studies tend to show that the worship of Yahweh as the only God must have become more significant in the late pre-exilic period in the southern kingdom of Judah, which already looked back to the collapse of the northern kingdom (722 B.C.) and was itself a vassal state of Ashur. It was explicitly raised to the status of a cultic norm under King Josiah, the religious reformer (in the closing years of the seventh century B.C.). This religious-political measure was probably preceded by forms of pressure from prophetic groups trying to implement sole worship of the God of Israel for various reasons and in different contexts. In this respect, they could certainly count on a self-evident acceptance of Yahweh at all levels of religious practice, from the temple cult of the capital, through the village sanctuaries, to family piety. Nevertheless, this traditional Yahweh worship was not monolatrous thoroughly, universally, or from the very start. For instance, various inscriptions,[8] but also biblical texts (2 Kgs 21.1–7), go to show that Yahweh was at least for a time honoured together with a female divinity as partner, and that this occurred in the royal temple. The hundreds of pillar figurines that have been found in houses and graves of the later kingship period are also thought to indicate the cult of a female divinity, in this instance honoured in family circles.

Therefore the prophetically-inspired transition – implemented under Josiah as a religious-political reform – from a traditional, non-polemical, and to a certain extent probably also monolatrous, Yahweh worship to a form of worship of Yahweh alone that explicitly excluded other cults (and was in this sense polemical) marks a decisive leap forward in the history of religion in Israel. Biblical texts, especially Deuteronomy, represent it as associated with the assumption of a linguistic and conceptual form that conceives of the relation of God to Israel by analogy with Assyrian vassalage contracts. As long as Israel diligently observes the Covenant and thereby gives proof of its love = loyalty to the Covenant, it will receive God's blessing; but if it breaks the

Covenant, it will call down on itself the curses bound up with the Covenant (Deut. 28.1–14; 15–68, and the entire structure of Deut. 5–28).

At this point we return to the Decalogue, which so to speak forms the preamble to the Covenant in Deuteronomy. The introductory verses of the Decalogue, more precisely translated (Deut. 5.6-7 / Exod. 20.2–3), are:

'I (am) Yahweh your God,
Who brought you out of the land of Egypt,
Out of the house of slavery.
There will be no other gods for you in opposition to me.'

The Decalogue does not begin with 'commandments' or 'prohibitions' but with Yahweh's identification of himself as the God who considers himself to be the God of Israel and who has delivered this people from a politically degraded, humiliating, and unjust situation. Israel ought not to be enslaved, and the God of Israel upholds its right to freedom. Israel's fundamental acknowledgement of its God is eminently political and is concerned with a nation's rights of self-determination and its rejection of colonialism. Moreover, the appended instructions to Israel are not formulated as a prohibition, but as a negative indicative ('thou shalt not' . . . = 'you are not going to . . .'). Here we find the expectation that, after experiencing God's liberating action, Israel can no longer do anything other than behave in accordance with this God's directions. Before all else, this implies an exclusive association with the God who has put an end to the enslavement of Israel. The God of Israel does not tolerate other gods, for they are 'in opposition' to him.

When we study the relation of the First Commandment to Yahweh's self-representation, it becomes clear that 'monotheism' is too imprecise a category to use in this instance,[10] for the deliverance of Israel from Egypt is cited as the point of reference, whereas we would expect the emphasis to be on God's creative power, as demanded by the traditional theological definition. But even the religious-historical category of monolatry would cover only one aspect of what is expressed here, since monolatry would refer only to religious practice and would elide the theological motivation for worship of Yahweh alone contained in God's self-representation. Consequently it would be more appropriate to describe the form of monolatry expressed at the beginning of the Decalogue as one that is soteriologically based, concentrated on the internal territory of Israel, and intolerant of other divinities.

This, however, reveals a paradox: the Decalogue acknowledges the God of Israel as the One who liberates it from slavery, yet, in the form of a preamble to a 'contract of vassalage', it transfers the pattern of the neo-Assyrian policy of subjection to the relationship between Israel and its God. Admittedly, this 'transposition of Assyrian despotism to God' would be an 'act of liberation that had made Israel independent of external despots'.[11] But then the God of Israel himself would acquire the characteristics of a despot who expects unconditional obedience from his subjects and punishes disobedient behaviour unmercifully – a conception of God that has also taken root in Christianity and has remained deeply embedded there.

III. Soteriological monotheism and the questioning of divine powers

The presentation is different in the texts of Deutero-Isaiah (Isa. 40–55):[12]

20 Assemble yourselves and come, draw near together, you survivors of the nations! They have no knowledge who carry about their wooden idols, and keep on praying to a god that cannot save.

21 Declare and present your case; let them take counsel together! Who told this long ago? Who declared it of old? Was it not I, Yahweh? And there is no other god besides me, a righteous God and a Saviour; there is none besides me.

22 Turn to me and be saved, all the ends of the earth! For I am God, and there is no other.

23 By myself have I sworn, from my mouth has gone forth in righteousness a word that shall not return: 'To me every knee shall bow, every tongue shall swear.'

24 Only in Yahweh, it shall be said of me, are righteousness and strength.
     . . .

(Isa. 45.20–24a)

In this text the assertion that there is no God other than the God of Israel is repeated three times (v. 21 twice; v. 22). Therefore the existence of other divinities is clearly rejected.[13] Consequently, recent exegetical monotheism research with reference to the texts of Deutero-Isaiah talks of the breakthrough of monotheism or of a 'theoretical' or 'reflective monotheism'.[14] In fact, the horizon of these texts, which must have originated from the closing years of the period of exile and under the impact of the collapse of the neo-Babylonian empire, extends far beyond that of the beginning of the Decalogue. The texts of Deutero-Isaiah portray the God of Israel as the

Lord of the most powerful political ruler of the world of his period, the Persian King Cyrus (cf. only 45.1ff). They thus encompass the world of all peoples and raise the power of the God of Israel to the level of a heavenly King of kings. They simultaneously proclaim the God of Israel as the creator of worlds, and extend the expanse of his power on a cosmic scale. The text from Isaiah 45 cited above also presents Yahweh as Lord over the ages. But the decisive criterion that declares that he is God is his power to save. Those who pray to gods who cannot save are ignorant (v. 20); Yahweh is the only God who is able to save (v. 21), and therefore those addressed are urged to turn to him from every corner of the earth to be saved (v. 22). The texts of Deutero-Isaiah are addressed to Israel especially. Isaiah 45.20–4 could also be addressed to Israelites in the diaspora, whom their God reminds that he is the only God who is able to save. But the formulations are also openly addressed to people outside Israel, perhaps even specifically to them,[15] and thus signify an invitation to the peoples of the world to entrust themselves to the saving power of the God of Israel, the one and only God, which upholds the world in justice.[16]

Accordingly, it is quite justifiable to describe the formulations of Deutero-Isaiah as 'monotheistic'. To be sure, they are not 'monotheistic' in the modern philosophical sense of focussing on the existence of a creator God transcendent to the world. They speak very specifically of God's action in history and assess God's divinity by his redemptive activity. Furthermore, these biblical texts are not concerned with the 'mere' existence of God or of other gods. Instead they conceive of the non-existence of other divinities in categories of power. The other gods (or the gods of others) are impotent and in that sense they do not exist. To that extent it is possible to talk of these texts as manifesting a 'dynamic soteriological monotheism'.

The rhetorical approach of these texts does not follow the Decalogue in seeing these other divinities as a provocation in the face of God, but distances itself from them derisively and in awareness of its own superiority. But the texts, never in any way doubting the incomparable greatness of the one God, also appeal to human intelligence (Isa. 45.20ff). They do not invoke obedient loyalty to a liege lord or use the fear of disasters as motivation, but rely on the evidence of the traces of God's action in the world. Theologically speaking, in the certainty that God's saving justice speaks the language of all humankind, this leaves the way and means open for every culture, and indeed every individual, to discover these traces of God.

IV. The integrative power of monotheism

A common feature of present-day reconstructions of the religious history of Israel is their acceptance of transformations of the 'identity' of the God of Israel. The oldest references by way of inscriptions from late Bronze Age Egypt lead us to suppose that Yahweh was originally a southern Palestinian tempest or weather god. This divinity underwent an initial decisive transformation as a result of its association with the city of Jerusalem and its temple in the early period of the Israelite kingship. The God of David and Solomon did not suppress the divinities honoured in Jerusalem but integrated their functions and in particular received the features of the sun god, whose main characteristic was the implementation of law and justice. This made a considerable change to the 'identity' of Yahweh. This kind of model of transformation by integration could offer prospects for discussion in dialogue between religions.

Old Testament scholarship also confirms the existence of transformation and integration in the period of the Second Temple, during which acknowledgement of the one unique God must already have affected considerable areas of the worship and piety of Israel. This profession of belief was also associated with, for instance, the notion that as King of the gods God is surrounded by a heavenly royal council or heavenly court. The references to the 'sons of God' found in some psalms and other hymnic and narrative texts (Ps. 29.1; 89.7; 82.6; Deut. 32.7-8; Gen. 6.1–4) can be integrated in this concept of a 'monarchical monotheism'. In the course of the transition of the Hebrew-biblical texts to the Greek linguistic and conceptual environment, the 'sons of God' became 'angels', heavenly intermediate beings acting as mediators between God and humans. This shows that the biblical 'monotheism' is not to be conceived of as in any way 'mono-lithic'.

Another form of integration of new features in the profile of the God of Israel in the post-exilic period is the literary personification of wisdom as a divine partner, 'at his side each day, his darling and delight', who was present when the world was created (Prov. 8.22ff). Thus, not only is the due ordering of the world expressed in the symbolic representation of a female figure, but the captivating aspect of female divinities is included in the conception of God. In addition to this female element mediated through the wisdom tradition, we find the attribution of maternal traits to Yahweh especially in the prophetic tradition (cf., in particular, Isa. 46.3ff; 49.15; 66.13 and Hos. 11).

In contrast to the supposition in early feminist theology that the presence of feminine symbols in the concepts of God advanced by a religious tradition would have directly positive implications for women's political and social situations, it is probably more prudent to assume the existence of more complex interactions between religious symbolic systems and social circumstances. Nevertheless, critical scrutiny of religious symbols is essential. Wherever, as in the Catholic tradition, it is considered appropriate to use the creation for analogy-formation when making statements about God, it is necessary to insist on the analogical appropriateness of female reality as well. Furthermore, wherever an iconocritical or negative theology is preferred, as in certain Protestant traditions, all anthropomorphic metaphors whatsoever that are used in discourse about God, including (or rather precisely) the main biblical metaphors, which in fact are drawn almost exclusively from a male symbolic world, must be included in any 'iconocritique' of this kind.[17]

V. 'Monotheism' and justice

The Deuteronomic-Deuteronomist tradition associated the worship of Yahweh alone with the theme of God's impatience, that of a jealous God who loves those who love him, and who punishes those who reject and hate him, as we read in the Decalogue (Deut. 5.9-10). If it is permissible to interpret the Decalogue as still monolatrous (that is, as recommending the worship of one God without denying the existence of other gods), other formulations, even in the Deuteronomic-Deuteronomist writings, go further and recall the 'reflective', or thoughtful, monotheism of Deutero-Isaiah, as in the account of the threat from the Assyrians under King Hezekiah (2 Kgs 19.14–19 / Isa. 37.15–20), and in Solomon's blessing of the whole assembly of the Israelites in Jerusalem (1 Kgs 8.60). The 'devouring fire' of God's jealousy (Deut. 4.24) appears in Moses' great address and proclamation of Deut. 4.1–40 as the reverse of the 'great fire', from the 'heart of which', that is, in the 'shape' of which, the God who is to be worshipped without making any image of him, and apart from whom there is no other God, appears (Deut. 4.32-9). Accordingly, it is not permissible simply to ascribe a greater potential for criticizing domination to 'reflective' monotheism than to a monolatrous way of thinking.

The early Jewish Books of the Maccabees, written or preserved in Greek, already tell us that an idea of God that takes account of his 'jealousy' can be adopted by human 'zealots', and can be expressed as acts of violence – inwardly as resistance, but also outwardly as civil war.[18] At all events, it is probably too simple an approach to assume a necessary connection between monotheistic beliefs and violent acts, for in all cases it is also a matter of complex series of events with a variety of causative factors that might favour a decision to exert violence in any specific instance. Furthermore, the example of the Books of the Maccabees should not mislead us into devolving the problem of religiously motivated violence onto Judaism. After all, it was Christianity in its early years that explicitly adopted the canon of the Septuagint and simultaneously these particular writings as its Bible, and it is Christianity that so very often in the course of its history has spread Christ's religion with fire and sword, and has persecuted 'heretics' within its own bounds with unremitting ferocity.

In any case, the concept and perception of violence certainly call for a highly nuanced approach. Finally, it is important in this respect to recall a criterion which the Hebrew Bible uses as a yardstick for God's divine nature and behaviour, and expresses succinctly in Psalm 82:[19]

1 God takes his place in the court of heaven
   to pronounce judgement among the gods:
2 'How much longer will you judge unjustly
   and favour the wicked?
3 Uphold the cause of the weak and the fatherless;
   and see right done to the afflicted and destitute.
4 Rescue the weak and the needy;
   and save them from the clutches of the wicked.'
5 But these gods know nothing and understand nothing,
   they walk about in darkness;
   meanwhile earth's foundations are all giving way.
6 'This is my sentence: Though you are gods,
   all sons of the Most High,
7 yet you shall die as mortals die,
   and fall as any prince does.'
8 God, arise and judge the earth,
   for all the nations are yours.

Clearly, in terms of the history of religions, the scenario of the psalm seems to be polytheistic. It presents us with a divine council or assembly of the sons of the highest God of all. Yet the Book of Psalms as a whole is a book directed to praise of, and appeals, petitions, and thanks to, the one unique God of Israel. We may understand texts such as that of Psalm 82 as having a mythologizing function in the post-exilic period, and in this instance as making explicit use of polytheistic wordplay. At all events, it is not unreasonable to suggest that Psalm 82 deals with and conveys experience of or with polytheism in Israel.

It appears, according to Psalm 82, that the divine council consists of the tutelary gods of all nations. One of the assembled divinities, called Elohim/God, takes his place in the court of heaven and addresses them. The overall context of the psalm shows that the God referred to here is the God of Israel. His speech is an accusatory oration or address by a prosecuting counsel, for the divine assembly becomes the scene of a court hearing. The peculiar aspect of this psalm is that here people are not brought to account, as often happens in the Hebrew Scriptures, but God pronounces judgment among the gods. The justice that must be worked is specific. It is a question of see-ing that right is done to those who have been treated unjustly, and even more precisely it is a matter of ensuring justice for those without intercessors: of paying for the defence of the destitute and needy, or of orphans who cannot call on their families for direct assistance. The sons of god who are called to judgment do not uphold this rule of compassion but permit or even favour the ill-treatment of the weak and afflicted. Therefore we hear the emphatic sentence that those sons of the Most High who do not support the weak but favour the wicked and their actions shall die as mortals die. They shall lose eternal life. The God who speaks thus is the only one to whom the criterion of aiding the weak applies, and so he is the Most High and the only God to obtain the designation Elohim=God. Therefore the last verse of the psalm also calls on him to arise and judge the earth.

Psalm 82 possesses a 'monotheistic' thrust, for the God of Israel exposes the national gods as no gods at all. This revelation occurs not in the shape of a murderous battle of the gods but takes the form of due judicial proceedings. Accordingly, the defining mark of (a) God's divinity is not a demonstration of his might in, say, war or the cosmos, but an ethical criterion, his concern that justice should be dispensed to those who cannot obtain justice by their own efforts. Whoever is not concerned to uphold the right of the wretched of the earth cannot be called God. Yet if the gods offend against this justice, the results are apparent not only in a human context but on a cosmic scale, for earth's foundations will all give way (cf. v. 5). Since, however, as the psalm tells us, only one God does indeed defend the right of the wretched, this criterion of God's divine behaviour also becomes a universal yardstick of justice embracing all the nations and the entire world.

On the other hand, this criterion has to be demonstrated ever and again because of the injustice that occurs in actual everyday life and in real situ-ations. The 'gods' who favour injustice in our present-day world must be redefined. Whoever has eyes to see will discover that the biblical God does not stand alone when contending for justice for the weak and needy, but has allies in the religions of humanity.

Translated by J. G. Cumming

Notes

1. See Lang (1995), Lemaire (2003), Zenger (2003, 2005) and Keel (2007) in the reading list below.
2. Cf. only Halpern (2008) and Finkelstein (2002).
3. See Wacker (2004) in this respect. The fact that the debate has not played any part (to date) in non-Western exegetical contexts may be related to the pronounced historical cast of its basic orientation, and to its association in the history of ideas with certain traditions of Western rational thought the significance of which is currently called in question (although that does not mean that this debate is irrelevant to the pertinent contexts).
4. Cf., especially, Finkelstein (2002).
5. Cf., e.g., Keel (2007) and Schroer (2006).
6. Assmann (2005), p. 38.
7. The Bible tells us nothing about the origins of polytheism. We can be certain only that the First Commandment assumes that polytheism is present in the world and environs of Israel.
8. The main instances are the inscriptions from Khirbet Qumran and Kuntillet Ajrud, which date from the middle kingdom.
9. Cf. also Moberly (2004) in this regard.
10. Cf. Assmann (2006), p. 24ff.
11. The recent exegesis of Isaiah certainly supports the independent origin of a basis for Isa. 40ff, but places much more emphasis on the weaving of this part of the text into the overall composition of Isaiah and the consequent treatment of the text. See Berges (2008) *passim*.
12. Cf. also Isa. 43.11; 45.5ff., 14; 46.9.
13. See, *e.g.*, Zenger (2005), p. 43 and *passim*, for the term 'reflective monotheism'.
14. Cf. Berges (2008), p. 431.
15. Paul related Isa. 45.23 both to the fact that we must all answer for our actions to God alone (Rom 14.11) and to the fact that in the end every tongue will confess that Jesus Christ is the Lord (cf. Phil 2.10ff).
16. Cf. Frettlöh (2006) as an instance of a systematic theological viewpoint in this regard.
17. Cf. Assmann (2006), p. 30ff with reference to 1 Macc. 3.3–9, 2 Macc 15, etc, which tell of the trust in God, valour, and noble effectiveness of Judas Maccabeus, who was 'like a lion in his deeds'.

18. See in this respect Kippenberg (2008), pp. 24ff and 206ff on the basis of his analyses of eight religiously motivated conflicts in recent years.
19. Cf. Zenger (2003), pp. 49ff; (2005), pp. 70ff; Wacker (2004), pp. 130ff.

Further reading

Jan Assmann, 'Monotheismus und die Sprache der Gewalt' in: Walter (2005), pp. 18–38

Ulrich Berges, *Jesaja 40–48*. Freiburg, 2008.

Israel Finkelstein & Neil Silberman *The Bible Unearthed*. New York, 2001.

Magdalene Frettlöh, *Gott Gewicht geben. Bausteine einer geschlechtergerechten Gotteslehre*. Neukirchen-Vluyn, 2006.

Baruch Halpern, *From Gods to God*. Tübingen, 2009.

André Lemaire, *Naissance du monothéisme. Vue d'un historien*. Paris, 2003.

Othmar Keel, *Jerusalem und der Monotheismus* (2 vols). Göttingen, 2007, esp. vol. 2, pp. 1270–82.

Hans Gerd Kippenberg, *Gewalt als Gottesdienst. Religionskriege im Zeitalter der Globalisierung*. Munich, 2008.

Bernhard Lang, 'Monotheismus', in: *Neues Bibel-Lexikon* II (1995), 834–44

Walter Moberly, 'How Appropriate is "Monotheism" as a Category for Biblical Interpretation?', in: Loren Stuckenbruck & Wendy E. S. North (eds), *Early Christian and Jewish Monotheism*. London & New York, 2004, pp. 216–34.

Marie-Theres Wacker, Der biblische Monotheismus – seine Entstehung und seine Folgen, in: Wacker (2004), pp. 105–37.

————, '"Monotheismus" als Kategorie der alttestamentlichen Wissenschaft. Erkenntnisse und Interessen', in: Wacker (2004), pp. 139–55

————, *Von Göttinnen, Göttern und dem einzigen Gott*. Münster, 2004.

Silvia Schroer (ed.), *Images and Gender. Contributions to the Hermeneutics of Reading Ancient Art*. Fribourg, 2006.

Peter Walter (ed.), *Das Gewaltpotential des Monotheismus und der dreieine Gott* (Questiones Disputatae 216). Freiburg, 2005.

Erich Zenger, 'Der Monotheismus Israels. Entstehung, Profil, Relevanz', in: Thomas Söding (ed.), *Ist der Glaube Feind der Freiheit? Die neue Debatte um den Monotheismus* (Questiones Disputatae 196). Freiburg, 2003, pp. 9–52

Erich Zenger, 'Der mosaische Monotheismus im Spannungsfeld zwischen Gewalt und Gewaltverzicht', in: Walter (2005), pp. 39–73.

The Unity of Revealed Law: The Torah and the Koran

JOSÉ LUIS SÁNCHEZ NOGALES

I. Monotheism

Judaism, Christianity, and Islam are prophetic monotheisms. The sum total of truths of faith professed by these three religions is very sensitive on this point. Their respective scriptures show the convergences and divergences in confession of monotheism. Judaism and Christianity designate God as Father,[1] which Islam rejects; Judaism and Islam converge in denying the mystery of the one and triune God, the nucleus of Christianity. Islam calls Jesus Messiah, which Judaism denies; both do not conceive of God as incarnate. Their theologies of 'revelation' do not coincide either. Judaism accords canonical status to the Torah and its rabbinical commentaries, the Talmud. Christianity closes revelation with the Apocalypse and the death of the last apostle: the revelation to the Jewish people is read and received in the light of the Christic alliance. For Judaism, the New Testament is not revealed truth. Although the Koran confers revelatory value on the Jewish and Christian scriptures, it nevertheless demotes them through the concept of *tahrīf*, the adulteration of these scriptures. Lately, a minority of Muslim thinkers have tried a new formulation: 'The *tahrīf* is the deviation undergone by the divine ray as it passes through the distorting prism of our imperfect humanity'.[2] Understood in this way, it would be accessible to Christianity; the problem is that it is not acceptable to Muslim orthodoxy, not can it be applied to its own book, the Koran.

Faith in one God alone can be predicated of the three great monotheisms.[3] This faith conceives the supreme reality with a personal character through the invocation of a proper name, which does not 'describe' God but makes relationship with him possible and prohibits his reification.[4] Strict monotheisms stress the exclusive sovereignty of God, which does not admit associated divinities or any break in oneness. But there are different accents: Judaism gives primacy to obedience and fulfilment of the Law, with a strong ethical component: 'listen and put what you have listened to into action'; Islam professes total submission to the will of God expressed in the Koran; in Christianity, love – corresponding to the love of God revealed in Christ – is the basic religious stance. The 'Abrahamic' monotheisms have adopted a polemical approach that, taken to its extreme, has led to various degrees of intolerance.[5] Monotheisms have a universalist calling: each one, separately and competitively, claims to be the one true religion for all humankind and the absolute religion in history.[6] Doctrinally and/or historically, they display a hierocratic tendency to constitute themselves as global and all-embracing systems, a clear characteristic of the prophetic monotheisms, though not exclusive to them: at some stage of their evolution they have tried to occupy the whole of human space, which has led to the clash of claims, to the oppression of religious minorities, and even to the justification of conflict and war by presenting them as the struggle of the God of some against the God of others.[7] But is this not one and the same God?

II. The '*eḥadia* of the Jewish creed

Current biblical exegesis detects signs that the Abraham of Genesis was not monotheist in the strict sense.[8] Yahweh was not yet the God of Abraham in Genesis, since the primacy of Yahweh begins with the covenant with Moses.[9] Judaism was to show itself progressively as strict and polemical monotheism.[10] What I call '*eḥadia* is its specific character, as found in the *šemà*: 'Hear, O Israel: Yahweh is our God, Yahweh alone ('*eḥad*). You shall love Yahweh your God with all your heart, and with all your soul, and will all your might' (Deut. 6.4–5). This 'alone' (one) is the Hebrew '*eḥad*, an adjective that basically means unique. Verse 5 contains the commandment to love God. The repetition makes it into a decisive point of Deuteronomist theology, the basic commandment that commits Israel to adoring Yahweh alone, and no other God. The context indicates that Deuteronomy 6.4. has to be interpreted in the light of this commandment and of the beginning of the Decalogue: for Israel, Yahweh is the one and only God. The existence of other gods is not denied, but the God Israel loves is the only one for Israel in all meanings of the term; this, though, is not yet strict monotheism.[12]

Exegetes are broadly agreed that Deuteronomy took over the previously adopted formula of *šemà*. The prophets were to take the Deuteronomic expression to its ultimate and radical consequences, denying that the gods of other nations had any validity or even existence.[13] The monotheistic faith nurtured by prophetic preaching grew during the Exile. Its paradigm is

perhaps the confession of Second Isaiah: 'I am the Lord, and there is no
other; beside me there is no god' (Isa. 45.5).[14] The reception of the *'eḥad*
is consolidated as a radical, strict, and polemical monotheism, which pro-
claims the nothingness of idols (41.24),[15] the exclusion of any divinity other
than Yahweh (44.6), Lord of creation and (44.24) and of history (40,15f).
The God of Israel is the only real one and excludes any other, the only God
beside whom there are no other gods, the total and indivisible in ontological
terms, absolutely simple and, at the same time, omnipresent. Later Judaism
would combat polytheism and idolatry, as shown in apocalyptic, rabbinic, and
inter-testamentary literature: its strongest line follows in the wake of Second
Isaiah declaring the nothingness of the gods.[16] It has a compact declaration of
faith in the formula *eís ó theós*.[17] The fundamental relationship in which this
'eḥadia is perceived in Judaism is that of salvation to creation. But the statement of God's oneness leads to the negation of any other god (Exod. 20.3).
Judaic *'eḥadia*, consolidated as strict monotheism would exclude polytheism,
dualism, and the divinity of Jesus.[18] The *Yigdal*, a liturgical hymn inspired
by the 'the thirteen articles of faith of Maimonides', sings of the divine oneness:

> Great is the living and exalted God;
> he exists and has no limit of time.
> He is one in his only oneness,
> hidden and infinite in his Unity (. . .).[19]

The formula 'denier of the Root' (*kofer ba 'iqqar*) from the mid-second
century designated one who denies the one God revealed to Israel; it was
applied to idolators, to those who deny that God is the creator, to those who
deny divine providence, and to the *minim*, persons familiar with the Jewish
concept of God but who alter it, including dualist Gnostics and Christians
who divinize Jesus. In missionary praxis, the first thing asked of the future
proselyte is abandonment of idolatry. Judaism rejects the existence of a mediator between God and humankind, but allows it to non-Jews, Christians, and
Muslims, provided they do not claim divine status for Jesus or Muhammad.
Judaism has, however, come to the conclusion that Christianity can be considered a permitted religion for non-Jews in accordance with God's plan.

III. The *aḥadia* of the Islamic profession of faith

Say: He is God, the Only (*aḥad*),
God the perfect, beyond compare.
He neither begets nor is begotten,
and in himself depends on no one (Koran 112.1–4).[21]

Lā ilāha Allāh wa-Muḥammadu rasūl Allāh, 'There is no god but God,[22] and Muhammad is the prophet (envoy) of God', is the formula of the *šahā da*. This confession of faith, continually present in the lives of Muslims, confirms Islam as one of the most theocratic religions. God is one and only (*aḥad*).[23] In the Islamic tradition the *šahāda* is *kalimaᵗ al-tawḥīd* (word of oneness) and the sura 112 quoted, called *al-ijlāṣ* (pure faith), is tradition-ally known as the *sūraᵗ al-tawḥīd* (sura of oneness). The term *tawḥīd* is not in the Koran as such, but the adjective *aḥad* and the numeral *wāḥid* are. The expression *ilāhun wāḥid* (the sole divinity) appears thirteen times, and the negative expression *lā ilāha illa huwa* (there is no god but Him) twenty-nine times. Muslims define themselves as *ahl al-tawḥīd* (people of oneness) and as *al-muwahhidūn* (unitarians).

This is a strict monotheism upheld not only against polytheists but also against Christianity and its doctrine of the Trinity. The exclusivity of the credal formula, with its initial 'no', forms a barrier against the greatest sin, never to be forgiven, of giving God associates. The Koran has theologized the origin of monotheism by going back to Abraham, whom it defines as *ḥanīf*: 'Abraham was neither Jew nor Christian, but was *ḥanīf* (*ḥanīfan*) subject to God (*muslīmān*) and not associator (*min al-mušrikīna*) (Koran 3.67).[24] Historically, Abraham cannot be considered a strict monotheist, but the Koran has made him into the model for polemical monotheism, in a process parallel to the one he underwent in biblical, inter-testamentary, and Talmudic literature.[25] In the Koran and in Islamic tradition, the term *ḥanīf* takes on the meaning of monotheist, sometimes synonymous with Muslim, as it is in the *aleya* (verse) quoted.[26] Ibn Maʿsūd[27] reads *ḥanīfiyya* in place of *islām* in Koran 3.19: 6: 'In truth, Religion (*dīn*), for God, is *islām* (or *ḥanīfiyya*)'. Those who do not practise this strict monotherism are called *mušrikūn*,[28] who commit the sin of *širk* (association) by putting gods next to God.[29]

Certain attributes are predicated of this one God that have given rise to problems in the – still unresolved – controversy between *muʿtazilíes* and *ašʿaríes*. The former – rationalists – identify these with the divine essence;

the latter – literalists – recognize their distinction from the divine essence, though without resolving the problem this poses for oneness. The same happens with the problem over the Koran, uncreated or created.[30] The first attribute defines God as wise creator (Koran 2.117), all-powerful, on whom all projects depend, so that *in šā' Allāh* (God willing) should be added to any statement referring to a future event or new orientation of thought. God cannot be called to account for what he does.[31] God is eternally transcendent, 'beyond our sight'.[32] God is inaccessible, indescribable; there is none like God,[33] and yet he is closer to us than our jugular vein,[34] but with the closeness of a master to his servant. The Koran rejects a God who became man and recognizes Jesus only as 'servant-adorer',[35] not a son of God,[36] nor the third of a triad, although it identifies Aaron and Moses' sister with the Virgin Mary and her with the third person of the Trinity.[37] Strictly speaking, the 'trinitarian' doctrine denied by the Koran is not Christian orthodoxy, although interpreters assure us that this Trinity is that denied on account of the 'irrefrangibility of the oneness' (*al-ṣamad*) of God.[38]

IV. *Eisity*: Trinity and incarnation of God

Mark 12.29–34 contains the *šemà* (Deut. 6.4–5) as Jesus' reply to a scribe's question: 'Hear, O Israel: the Lord our God, the Lord is one' [. . .][39] 'You are right, Teacher; you have truly said that "he is one, and besides him there is no other"' [. . .].[40] The word used in the two mentions of oneness is *eîs*.[41] The New Testament accepts the monotheist confession of Israel. Jesus calls the scribe's statement excluding the existence of any god besides God as 'wise'. I call this quality of oneness '*eisity*', from the Greek translation of the *'eḥ ad* of the Hebrew Bible. I prefer this root to the Johannine *mónos*,[42] because this has the connotation of solitary and isolated; which is, in another sense, an advantage. The New Testament confesses God's oneness in the sense the *šemà* acquired as monotheism was consolidated. The fullness of monotheism was reached in the understanding of the first commandment: not to place any idol beside God,[43] or cosmic powers or worldly authorities.[44] Jesus' *eîs* of the *šemà* underlines the total exclusion between God and all 'anti-god', since a servant can serve only one master (Matt. 6.24). The New Testament *eîs* is contextualized in an organic and dynamic thinking in which Christ forms one unity with the Father and leads his community so 'that they may become completely one (*èn*)' (John 17.23).[45] Christian monotheism is experienced as listening to God, trusting in him, faithfulness even to martyrdom: this is how Jesus and the earliest Christians understood monotheism.[46] To the man who called him 'Good Teacher', Jesus replied, 'No one is good but God alone.'[47] At the same time he maintains his claim to divine sonship (Mark 1.1; 14.61, par.), calling God his Father (Mark 14.36). In the same way his association with the Spirit of God is shown in the scene of his Baptism (Mark 1.11) and in a special way in John's Gospel, in which Jesus makes a distinction: he speaks not of 'our Father' but of 'my Father and your Father . . . my God and your God' (20.17). He is the Son, who rejects the temptations of the evil one, who calls him 'son of God', appealing to God as alone worthy of worship, following the profession of Deuteronomy 6.13. The lordship of the one and only God is confirmed in him and with him. Jesus speaks of God as 'the God of Abraham, Isaac, and Jacob' (Mark 12.26–7, par.) and identifies his Father with the God of the Jews (John 8.42). The New Testament preaches a strict monotheism, including Jesus' claim to belonging in the mystery of God. Who sees him, sees the Father (John 14.9), with whom he is one (*eîs:* John 10.30; 17.11, 21ff). In the Gospels, especially John's, Jesus speaks in the first person in the manner of God. The formula *egô eími* without a predicate carries echoes of the God of the Old Testament.

Christianity, from this revealed base, stresses the differentiated oneness of God, which constitutes God's life and inner dynamism and leads him to cross the abyss that separates him from mankind in the incarnation. God is Father of all. Jesus reveals him and reveals himself as God's Son. After his death and resurrection, the first Christians would define God as love (1 John 4.8). Their experience of community and christological reflection would translate this inner life of love as interchange among the three divine Persons. Besides emphasizing the relationship of Jesus the Son to the Father in oneness (1 Cor. 8.6). the New Testament stresses Jesus' relationship with the Spirit of God. The overall picture of these relationships finds its expression in the formula *kyrios, theós, pneûma* (2 Cor. 3.13) or *pneûma, kyrios, theós* (1 Cor. 12.4–6); the formula *pathr, yiós, pneûma* appeared in Matthew 28.19.[48] God never sheds his oneness or his transcendence. The Christian faith sees itself as faithful to the oneness of God, even though this oneness in understood in a different way from that in which it is in Judaism and Islam. These seem to approach more of a mathematical-arithmetical concept of oneness, even approximate to what could be called a deduction from philosophical reasoning.

In Christian faith, no hiatus can be introduced between Jesus and God. Christians, not without divine help, have overcome the scandal of impotence and foolishness in the realm of human perception.[49] To overcome the scandal, one has to go through its very heart. If theological solutions from faith attempt to dissimulate the real difference, to avoid confrontation with the scandal, they have then lost sight of their mission.

Jews and Muslims do not accept the mystery of Jesus as God. This is a sufficiently solid reality to impel Christian theologians to examine our beliefs for the living coherence of our faith at a time when we are embarking on the risky adventure of dialogue. Jews and Muslims sometimes set us an example of transparency in their profession of faith. Of course I am not referring here to theological positions so rigid that they border on the fanaticism that threatens the death of faith itself while at the same time making any dialogue impossible. The Jewish Pinchas Lapide's reply to Hans Küng makes this clear: 'Theologizing from below, we can journey together for thirty-three years, the duration of Jesus' life on earth, and this is no small thing. What really separate us are the forty-eight hours from the evening of the first Good Friday. They are only two days, but they are just the decisive days on which the whole of christology depends'.[50] If these 'forty-eight hours' were to designate the Easter experience, I could come close to Lapide's phrase, though I would introduce some modifications into it.

We believe in one sole God.[51] Does this guarantee the ontological identity of the God confessed? There is no doubt about the continuity between the Yahweh of the Jews and the Father of Jesus. The Koran accepts the continuity of its God – whose word it claims to be contain – with that of the God proclaimed by Jews and Christians.[52] This acceptance in the Koran – which the most traditional interpretation in any case denies – is not considered by Catholic theology to constitute a source of theological authority: 'They share the same God. But this does not mean that the concept of God is identical in the three monotheistic religions. At least on the doctrinal level, the opposite is the case.'[53] God is recognized as one and only: this propels us to mutual respect, to dialogue in a genuine spirit, and to the convergent witness we can and must give. In this dialogue, we Christians cannot omit the profession of our faith: what we Christians have been able to know of God we have received through God's self-communication in Jesus Christ, only-begotten Son of the Father, sealed with the power and the strength of the Spirit of God.

Translated by Paul Burns

Notes

1. Cf. A. Rodríguez Carmona, 'Dios Padre revelado en Cristo Jesús', in *El Dios y Padre de Nuestro Señor Jesucristo*, Pamplona, 2000, p. 34–42.
2. Cf. GRIC, *Ces Écritures qui nous questionnent. Bible & Coran*, Paris: Cerf, 1987, pp. 126–34.
3. J. Martín Velasco, *Introducción a la fenomenología de la religión*, Madrid: Trotta, 2006, p. 323; Cf. pp. 323–48.
4. Cf. B. Welte, *Religionsphilosophie*, Freiburg: Herder, 1978. Here Sp. trans., *Filosofía de la Religión*, 1982, p. 122ff.
5. Cf. K. J. Kuschel, *Discordia en la casa de Abrahán. Lo que separa y lo que une a judíos, cristianos y musulmanes*, Estella: Verbo Divino, 1996, pp. 110–84.
6. Cf. J. Dupuis, *Vers une théologie chrétienne du pluralisme religieux*, Paris: Cerf, 1977. Here Sp. trans., 2000, p. 338–45.
7. Cf. Welte, *Filosofía de la Religión, op. cit.* pp. 155–6.
8. Cf. Kuschel, *Discordia, op. cit.,* pp. 275–319.
9. Cf. 'jhwh': *Theologishes Wörterbuch zum Alten Testament* III, 547-554.
10. Cf. H. Küng, *El Judaísmo. Pasado, presente y futuro*, Madrid: Trotta, 1993, pp. 41–4 and 48–9.
11 NRSV (adapted). Masoretic text: 'YHWH ʾelhºyºnw YHWH ʾeḥad'.
12. Cf. 'ehad': *Theologishes Wörterbuch zum Alten Testament* I, 211–18.
13. Cf. J. Martín Velasco, *Introducción a la fenomenología, op. cit.* pp. 330–41.
14. Isa. 45.5: 'ᵃny YHWH ʷʾeyn ʾwd zwlatay ʾeyn ʾᵉelohym'.
15 'You indeed are nothing, and your work is nothing at all' (hen-'attem me'yn wfa'alkhem me'afa').
16. 'Theós': *Theologisches Wörterbuch zum Neuen Testament* III, 398–409.
17. Cf. Zech 14. 9: 'kyrios eîs kaì tò ónoma aútoū 'hn'.
18. Cf. Küng, *El Judaísmo, op. cit.,* pp. 300–07.
19. B. Bayer, 'Yigdal', in *Encyclopaedia Judaica* 16, 833–5.
20. Cf. R. A. Kaplan, *Précis de la pensée juive*, New York and Jerusalem: Moznaïm Publishing Corp. – Arche du livre, 1994, p. 3.
21. J. Cortés, *El Corán*, Intro. J. Jomier, Barcelona: Herder, 1999, bilingual edition.
22. Koran 37.5.
23. Cf. 'Allah': *Encyclopédie de l'Islam. Nouvelle édition* I, Maisoneuve *et al.*, Paris 1960, pp. 419, 422–4.
24. *Ḥanīf* in the singular: Koran 2.135; 3.67,95; 4.125; 6.79,161; 16.120,123; 22.3; 50.32.
25. Cf. 'Genesis Rabba' 38.11, 28, in *Midrash Rabba. Genesis I-II*, London and New York, ³1983. pp. 310–11. Parallels to 'Genesis Rabba': Koran 21.51–67; 37.91–8. Cf. J. L. Sánchez Nogales, *Abrahán y los pueblos bendecidos*, Almería: Centro de EE. Eccos, 2005, pp. 8–17; 28–42.
26. Cf. W. Montgomery Watt, 'Hanif': A. T. Khoury – L. Hagemann, *Dictionnaire de l'Islam*, Turnhout: Brepols, 1995, pp. 250f.

27. Cf. A. Jeffery, *Materials for the history of the text of the Qur'an*, Leiden: E. J. Brill, 1937, p. 32.
28. Cf. Koran 2.165, 221; 4.48, 116; 16.35; 31.13; 39.45–6;
29. Cf. L. Hagemann, 'Dieu (Allāh)': A. T. Khoury and L. Hagemann, *Dictionnaire de l'Islam, op. cit.*, p. 117.
30. Cf. L. Gardet, 'Dieu, Le Réel (Allāh al-hāqq)', *Studia Missionalia* 17 (1968), 67–8.
31. Cf. Koran 2.107, 115; 3.189; 4.131–4, 139; 7.185; 22.61–6; 28.71–5; 36.78–83; 39.62–3; 40.57-65; 41.37–40; 53.43–62.
32. Cf. Koran 6.103.
33. Cf. Koran 42.11; 17.42–3; 21.22.
34. Cf. Koran 50.16.
35. Cf. Koran 43.57–9.
36. Cf. Koran 5.72, 116–7.
37. Cf. Koran 5.116; 4.171–2; 5.73.
38. Koran 112.1–3.
39. 'kyrios ò theós hemōn kyrios eîs éstin'.
40. 'eís éstin kaì oúk eis éstin'állos plhn aútoū'.
41. The formula *eís theós* appears in Rom. 3.29–30; Gal. 3.20; Eph. 4.6; 1 Tim. 2.5; James 2.19; 1 Cor. 8.4–5, etc.
42. The formula *mónos theós* appears in 1 Tim. 1.17; Jude 25; John 17.3; Rom. 16.27.
43. Cf. Matt 6,24; Mark 10.21; Luke 12.19ff; 1 Cor. 10.21; 2 Cor. 6.16; Phil. 3.19.
44. Cf. Gal. 4.8ff; Acts 4.19; 5.29; Mark 12.17.
45. Cf. 'Eís': *Teologisches Wörterbuch zum Neuen Testament*, II, 432–40.
46. Cf. 'Theós': *ibid.*, IV, 101–2.
47. Mark 10.18: *oúdeis ágathós eí mh eîs theós*.
48. Cf. 'Theós, *art. cit.*, 104–5; 'Ego', *idem* III, 66ff.
49. Cf. 1 Cor. 1.22–4.
50. H. Küng, *El Judaísmo, op. cit.*, p. 301.
51. Cf. J. Dupuis, *Vers une théologie chrétienne, op. cit*, Sp. trans. pp. 380–8.
52. Cf. Koran 29.46.
53. Dupuis, *Vers une théologie chrétienne, op. cit.*, Sp. trans. p. 385.

Theism and Tolerance in Hinduism

CATHERINE CORNILLE

Introduction

In discussions on religious pluralism and tolerance, Hinduism is extolled as the prime example of a religion able to coexist peacefully with other religious traditions, both in its own homeland of India and abroad. Few religious wars have been waged in the name of 'Hinduism', and Hindus have on the whole posed little resistance to the entry or rise of other religions within their own religious context. Even though this image of Hinduism has been somewhat tainted by the emergence of Hindu nationalism and the recent violence against 'foreign' religions, these developments tend to be regarded as deviations from the true and authentic tradition, which is seen as essentially welcoming and tolerant of the religious other. This tolerance may be attributed – both positively and negatively – to the internal diversity of the Hindu tradition. Hinduism indeed encompasses a large variety of different beliefs and practices, from various forms of theism to the radical rejection of the existence of a personal God, and from practices of intense and passionate devotion to severe asceticism and reliance on one's own yogic powers. The lack of unity and centralized authority within Hinduism may be seen to preclude any concerted action against other religious traditions. In so far as the very term 'Hinduism' as denoting a distinct religion has been generally recognized to be a modern and Western invention, there was traditionally little common ideological ground to defend against or impose upon religious others. While this internal diversity may be regarded negatively as a weakness, it may also be viewed more positively as a strength, as the very basis for recognizing diversity outside of the tradition. Hindu tolerance toward other religions is then grounded in its tolerance toward a variety of belief systems within, and in its experience with making theological or philosophical sense of religious diversity. Indeed, many of the theological models that have been developed in the past few decades to make sense of religious diversity in the West (inclusivism, exclusivism, pluralism) have a long history in India.

In terms of its internal diversity, it is the absence of a common belief in one God that is often regarded as the main reason for Hindu tolerance toward other religions. However, such generalization does not do justice either to the Hindu tradition or to the argument about the connection between monotheism and violence.[1] While it is true that none of the gods of Hinduism has been able to gain universal and unique recognition in India, Hinduism certainly includes strong theistic and even monotheistic traditions, both traditional and modern. One finds in fact throughout Hindu scriptures various attempts to maintain a balance between a recognition of diversity and a search for unity of the ultimate reality. This unity is at times found in a personal God and at times in a non-personal ultimate reality. Hinduism therefore offers an interesting test-case for the relationship between monotheism and intolerance. Is it the case that the monotheistic traditions of Hinduism have been less tolerant of religious other than the non-theistic ones? What has been the role of theism and monotheism in the developments of Hindu nationalism and antagonism toward other religions?

I. The one and the many

The Hindu pantheon has always been populated with a large number of gods. While the early Vedic gods tended to be associated with natural phenomena: lightning (Indra), dawn (Usas), the sky (Dyaus), night (Nirriti), the sun (Surya), the later gods of the Puranas came to assume a more anthropomorphic form. Most of the male gods in the Hindu pantheon were depicted with female counterparts or consorts, while some female goddesses also came to be worshipped as independent deities. Some gods were regarded as benevolent and others as more ambivalent. Some deities were associated with specific locations, and with particular needs, while others acquired a more pan-Indian devotion and universal power. The three main gods worshipped in India today are Śiva, Vishnu, and Devi. Śiva is the God of destruction and recreation, the patron saint of ascetics as well as the god of lovers, in short, the god who combines all opposites. His mythology associates him with different goddesses (Satī, Pārvatī, and Kali) and his iconography depicts him as lord of the dance (Śiva *natarāja*), as phallic symbol (Śiva-lingam), and as the great ascetic. His son Ganesha (the god with the elephant head) is also worshipped throughout India as the god who removes obstacles and assists devotees through various situations of transition. The god Vishnu is portrayed as the preserver, and often worshipped through his *avatāras* or incarnations, believed to descend to the world in times of crises to save it from destruction. The most famous of Vishnu's incarnations are Rāma and Krishna, who are themselves accompanied by their consorts, Sītā and Rādhā. Among the independent female Gods, Durga and Kali deserve particular mention. Both are depicted as fierce and victorious in battle. But while Durga is portrayed as an attractive Goddess, Kali is represented as fearful, wild, and bloodthirsty. These and many other Goddesses tend to be associated with nature, and with the cause and cure of diseases.[2]

The debate over how to typify this pantheon of Hindu Gods and Goddesses has been ongoing. While many missionaries described (and denounced) the multiplicity of Gods worshipped in India as plain polytheism, early scholars of Hinduism such as Friedrich Max Müller coined the term henotheism to denote the successive worship of one God at a time as the highest. In *The Wonder that was India*, A. L. Basham speaks of the Hindu Gods as 'a diamond of innumerable facets; two very large and bright facets are Vishnu and Śiva, while the others represent all the Gods that were ever worshipped. Some facets seem larger, brighter, and better polished than others, but in fact the devotee, whatever his sect, worships the whole diamond, which is in reality perfect.'[3]

This search for unity behind the multiplicity of Gods was more than a Western scholarly imposition on Hinduism. Hindu texts themselves from the beginning suggest an awareness of a unifying principle underlying the diversity of divine names and forms.

This is evident already in the Rg Veda, which states that ' They call it Indra, Mitra, Varuna, and Agni, . . ., but the real is one, although the sages give different names' (Rg Veda 1.169). The text also displays a playful attitude about the number of Gods, counting them variously at 3,003 or 303 or 3 (Rg Veda 3.9.9). All of these Gods are moreover seen to derive from one originating principle, variously thought to be the creative word (Vac) or the God of sacrifice (Prajāpati). In the Upanishads (800–200 BC) this search for unity is pursued by focusing on the one ultimate reality underlying all existence (Brahman), conceived of now in personal and then in non-personal terms. This led to the development of various theistic and non-theistic philosophical schools within classical Hinduism. Whereas theistic philosophers and religious thinkers (Rāmānuja, Nimbārka, Mādhva, Vallabha) may have differed in their conception of the relationship between God, the world, and the Self, each maintained a focus on one God, though varying from one to the next.[4] In Hindu mythology, the unity or relationship between the main Gods in the Hindu pantheon is at times expressed in terms of the Trimurti, or three manifestations of God as creator (Brahma), preserver (Vishnu) and destroyer (Śiva). However, each tradition also came to regard its own God as superior to or more powerful than the others. This was also reflected in the Hindu pattern of worship, which tended to focus on one particular god who became the object of particular devotion. Even though the Hindu tradition distinguishes village gods (*grāma-devata*), family gods (*kula-devata*) and gods of personal choice (*iśtha-devata*), these gods tended to be one and the same in the religious life of devotees, the village god often becoming the family god, and the family god becoming one's personal god.

In spite of the multiplicity of gods worshipped in India, some scholars thus speak categorically of the presence of monotheism in Hinduism. Friedhelm Hardy, for example, sees the root of Hindu monotheism in the appearance (probably abound the fourth century BC) of the notion of Bhagavān as 'a single, all-powerful, eternal, personal and loving God', serving as an 'empty slot, to be filled by concrete characteristics which then make up a specific Bhagavān-figure who serves as (the one and only) God to a given group of people.'[5] This, according to Hardy, developed into a 'blatantly monotheistic' system in the work of Rāmānuja, culminating in the *Rāmcharitmānas* of Tulsidas (sixteenth century), where Rāmā is regarded as Bhagavān, and not merely as an *avatāra* of Vishnu.[6] Focus on a particular god led to the development of a veritable sectarianism in the history of Hinduism,[7] and at times to competition between different sectarian groups. In modern times, the search for a unified conception of God has often been related to the desire for a clear and defined Hindu identity in relation to pressures from other religious traditions.

II. Monism, monotheism, and tolerance

The proverbial tolerance of Hinduism is generally connected less to the theistic than to the monistic or non-dualistic traditions of Hinduism. The classical image (at least in the West) of Hindu tolerance is that of the various religious traditions as different paths leading to the same ultimate peak. The peak represents the ultimate reality which is beyond all understanding, but which different religions call by various names. This image fits within the non-dualistic worldview of Advaita Vedanta, which distinguishes between the one ultimate reality beyond all conception (Nirguna Brahman) and the various qualified representations of that reality (Saguna Brahman). The different conceptions of God and the different religious paths may thus be regarded as various interpretations of the infinite and ineffable ultimate reality. It is this 'freedom of interpretation' that, according to the Indian philosopher and statesman Sarvapelli Radhakrishnan, is responsible for 'the hospitality of the Hindu mind.'[8] It allows for a recognition of various religious traditions as ultimately pointing to the same transcendent truth. The question as to whether this constitutes genuine tolerance and hospitality is open to debate. Gavin D'Costa argues that, in so far as it reduces other religions to its own conception of ultimate reality and fails to recognize them in their own self-understanding, it may be regarded as a form of exclusivism.[9] However, one cannot deny the fact that Hindu monism has rarely in itself fuelled attitudes of aggression or violence toward other systems of belief, both within and beyond Hinduism.

While Hindu tolerance may thus be seen to originate from a non-theistic conception of ultimate reality, it is far from incompatible with the more theistic and even monotheistic traditions of India. Many of the Hindu temples dedicated to one particular God also include statues of other Gods, though less prominently displayed. And even though one certainly finds vigorous debates between the different sectarian traditions of Hinduism, these in fact rarely led to bloodshed. This attitude of religious tolerance among different theistic traditions may be attributed to a Vedic legacy of polytheism or henotheism, or to a long tradition of vacillation between unity and diversity in the Hindu conception of the divine. But it may also be seen to be grounded in a more reflective theological stance, which is almost as old as Hindu theism itself. In the *Bhagavadgītā*, one of the founding texts of the Hindu belief in God, Krishna offers what may be regarded as one of the oldest examples of religious inclusivism. The text first of all emphasizes the unity, supremacy and all-pervasiveness of God:

> Nothing is higher than I am;
> Arjuna, all that exists
> is woven on me,
> like a web of pearls on thread. (7:7)

> He who sees me everywhere
> and sees everything in me
> will not be lost to me,
> and I will not be lost to him. (6:30)

> I exist in all creatures,
> so the disciplined man devoted to me
> grasps the oneness of life;
> wherever he is, he is in me. (6:31)

Even though the text presents the ultimate goal of life and the ultimate means
to salvation in terms of knowledge of and surrender to Krishna/Vishnu, it
also acknowledges the reality of devotion to other Gods. Rather than reject
such devotion, the text describes it as ultimately pointing to Krishna, whether
or not people are aware of it:

> When devoted men sacrifice
> To other deities with faith,
> They sacrifice to me, Arjuna,
> However aberrant the rites. (9:23)

> I grant unwavering faith
> To any devoted man who wants
> To worship any form
> with faith. (7:20)

> Disciplined by that faith,
> He seeks the deity's favor;
> Thus secured, he gains desires
> That I myself grant. (7:21)

Krishna is here thus regarded as the ultimate source and goal of all devotion,
regardless of its object. The value of the worship of other Gods is not denied,
since all acts of devotion are considered to be fruit of the grace of Krishna.[10]
But the faulty designation of these other Gods, and the distortion of the
ritual are regarded as the fruit of ignorance:

> Robbed of knowledge by stray desires,
> Men take refuge in other deities;
> Observing varied rites,
> They are limited by their own nature. (7:20)

This sheds some light on how one might understand Hindu tolerance in the
context of its belief in God. It is not a tolerance which is based on recognition
of the equality or the equivalence of other conceptions of God. Rather, it is
based on a clear sense of the superiority or uniqueness of one's own divine
expression, combined with a recognition that God's grace is also operative
beyond the confines of one's own devotional tradition. It may thus be seen
to lead to a certain domestication of the religious other, and to reflect an atti-

tude of condescension, both critiques which have also been levelled against other forms of religious inclusivism. However, it does point to the fact that monotheism does not necessarily or inherently engender attitudes of aggression and violence against other religions.

III. Monotheism and violence

Even though monotheism has rarely led to violence in the history of Hinduism, the cases where it has offer illuminating examples of the ways in which monotheism can be used or abused to bring about tension between different religious groups. Though occasional outbursts of violence are recorded between orthodox Hindus and so-called heretics (usually referring to Ajīvikas, Jains and Tantrikas),[11] the main evidence of religious aggression dates from the modern period. Various scholars have written about the emergence of warrior ascetics in medieval India.[12] These ascetics were generally related to one or another temple or monastery, and assigned with the defence of its property and income against the whims of a particular ruler or antagonism from other traditions (*sampradāyas*). In times of scarce resources and/or political tension, each tradition was forced to fend for its own interests and rights. It appears that most of the tension between the different sects was 'over the policing of the great religious fairs and the collection of pilgrim dues.'[13] Conflict also at times arose from the political support of one or the other religious group. In *Le Trident sur le Palais*, Catherine Clémentain-Ojha discusses the case of the actual royal persecution of Vaisnavas in the state of Jaipur in the middle of the nineteenth century.[13] In order to curb the power and wealth of Vaisnavas, Rāmsingh II converted to Śaivism and forced Vaisnavas to wear the Śaiva forehead marks. Such acts of religious violence were however rare in the history of Hinduism and were clearly inspired by political and economic interests.

In the recent history of India, one also finds attempts to use monotheism to strengthen Hindu identity and unity, often in reaction to a sense of threat from other religions, in particular Christianity and Islam. In the course of the nineteenth century, vigorous debates took place over the true nature of Hinduism. Hindu reformers tended to emphasize the fact that Hinduism was essentially monotheistic, but opinions differed over which god was to be regarded as the one god of all Hindus. Vasudha Dalmia recounts how various attempts were made in the nineteenth century to unify the various Vaisnava Sampradāyas under the worship of one God: śrirādhāraman.[14] Supported by Western Orientalists (Monier Williams, Grierson), Vaisnavism was por-

trayed as both the oldest and the main religion of India, and ultimately as the
origin of all religions. This, however, was directly countered by attempts, as
mentioned above, to place Śiva at the center of Hindu devotion. Rather than
advance one or the other existing god as the God of all Hindus, some have
in more recent times attempted to bring about unity by creating a new type
of divinity. In *Divine Enterprise*, for example, Lisa McKean discusses the
erection in the 1980s of the Bharat Mata temple in Hardwar.[15] The divinity
worshipped in this temple is based on Bankim Chandra Chatterji's famous
novel *Anandamath*. Though the temple includes statues and references to
all the major gods, heroes, and saints of India, the Goddess, identified with
mother India, functions as the main point of unity and worship. This devotion contributed to the ability of Hindu militants to create a sense of religious
nationalism and to galvanize aggression against foreign religions. It created,
as Mckean puts it, a band of 'militant Matriots . . . who, ever eager to assert
their devotion, readily construe events as offences against Bharat Mata.'[16]
The main intention behind the development of this type of monotheism
was thus clearly that of unifying all Hindus against Muslims and Christians.
The sad results of this type of theism are obvious: thousands of people have
been killed in various riots, unleashed to 'defend' Hinduism against foreign
occupations. Any type of perceived critique of Hinduism has been met with
violence and a proclaimed need to preserve the integrity of Hindu faith.
While many of the reasons or causes of this type of religious fundamentalism
and aggression may be attributed to structural causes similar to those which
have come to explain fundamentalism in other parts of the world, the fact
remains that the development of a common deity for all Hindus helped to
galvanize feelings of aggression toward other religious communities.

Conclusion

Rather than as a model of religious tolerance, Hinduism may be regarded
as a microcosm of religious ideas and practices and as an illustration of how
monotheism may be used to generate both tolerant and intolerant attitudes
toward the religious other. The search for unity in diversity in the Hindu
tradition led to the development of various strands of theism and monotheism, alongside monistic schools of thought. In has become clear that in
Hinduism, monotheism may lead, no less than monism, to genuine tolerance
toward other religious traditions. While for monism, this tolerance is based
on the notion of the ineffability of the ultimate reality and on the reality of
ignorance, monotheistic traditions ground it in the belief in the supremacy

of one's own god and in the idea that all true faith is unwittingly derived from and oriented toward this god. In both cases, tolerance is thus less a matter of recognizing the distinctiveness and equivalence of other religious paths, than of subsuming them within one's own conception of ultimate truth. While this form of 'domestication' of the religious other may be regarded as a distortion of the self-understanding of the other (which it certainly is), it must also be regarded as a religiously coherent and relatively peaceful way of coming to terms with the reality of religious diversity. It has become the standard way of dealing with the existence of other religions in most religious traditions. And it has rarely led to religious violence.

Even though the Hindu tradition thus offers a clear example of the compatibility of monotheism and tolerance, it also reminds us of the aggressive and intolerant potential of monotheistic beliefs. The warrior ascetics were certainly not unique to monotheistic traditions. One also finds them among the monistic (Dasānamī) orders. But it is clear that monotheistic beliefs lent themselves more readily to exclusivist interpretations,[17] and to attitudes of animosity toward other religious groups. As such, Vaisnavas and Śaivas did at times vie with one another for supremacy and dominance, and the tension between the two traditions was occasionally exploited for political interest. And in present-day India, a new type of monotheism has been invented in order to unify all Hindus against religious others. While monotheism does not naturally or necessarily lead to religious intolerance and violence, Hinduism thus also offers an example of how the thirst for violence may be fuelled by monotheistic beliefs and how monotheism may be manipulated for economical, political, and indeed also religious purposes.

Notes

1. In my book *The Im-Possibility of Interreligious Dialogue* (New York: Crossroad/ Herder & Herder, 2008), I argue that a proper understanding of monotheism, or belief in a unifying transcendent reality as the source of all goodness and truth in other religions, may in fact be a condition, rather than an impediment to dialogue (pp. 127–45).
2. For more on the Hindu goddesses, see Tracy Pintchman, *Rise of the Goddess in the Hindu Tradition*, Albany: SUNY Press, 1994; Friedhelm Hawley and Donna Wulff, *The Divine Consort: Rādhā and the Goddesses of India*, Berkeley: University of California Press, 1982; Heidi Pauwels, *The Goddess as Role Model. Sītā and Rādhā in Scripture and on Screen*, Oxford: Oxford University Press, 2008.
3 A. L. Basham, *The Wonder that was India*, New York: Grove Press, 1954, p. 309.

4. For Rāmānuja, this was the pair Vishnu-Laksmi, for Nimbarka the pair Krishna-Rādhā, for Nimbārka Vishnu, and for Vallabha Krishna.

5. Friedhelm Hardy, 'The Classical Religions of India', in *The World's Religions: The Religions of Asia*, London: Routledge, 1988, p. 79.

6. *Ibid.*, pp. 93, 111.

7. Śrī-Vaisnavas, Śaiva Siddhāntas, Lingāyats, Vīraśaivas, Pancarātras, Vaikhā nasas, Pāsupatas, Kāpālikas, etc.

8. Sarvapelli Radhakrishnan and Charles Moore, *A Sourcebook in Indian Philosophy*, Princeton: Princeton University Press, 1957, p. 624.

9. For a critique of this position as a form of religious 'exclusivism' see Gavin D'Costa, *The Meeting of Religions and the Trinity*, Maryknoll, NY: Orbis Books, 2000, pp. 56–71.

10. Religious traditions focused on the *Bhagavadgītā*, such as the International Society for Krishna Consciousness, thus have less difficulty recognizing other theistic traditions, even outside the Hindu fold, than they do recognizing non-theistic traditions even within Hinduism.

11. See Wendy D. O'Flaherty, 'The Origin of Heresy in Hindu Mythology', in *History of Religions* X, 1971, pp. 271–333.

12. For a classical discussion of Indian warrior ascetics see the classic article by David Lorensen, 'Warrior Ascetics in Indian History', *Journal of the American Oriental Society*, vol. 98 (1978).

13. Lorenzen here quotes W. G. Orr, 'Armed Religious Ascetics in Northern India', *Bulletin of the John Rylands Library* XXIV (1949), p. 88.

14. Catherine Clémentin-Ojha, *Le Trident sur le Palais: Une Cabakka Anti-Vishnouite dans un Royaume Hindou à l'Époque Coloniale*, Paris: Presses de l'Ecole Française de l'Extrême-Orient, 1999.

15. See Vasudha Dalmia, *The Nationalization of Hindu Traditions*, Delhi: Oxford University Press, 1997, p. 367.

16. Lise McKean, *Divine Enterprise. Gurus and the Hindu Nationalist Movement*, Chicago: University of Chicago Press, 1996.

17. *Ibid.*, p. 147.

'You truly see the Trinity where you see love'
(St Augustine, *De Trinitate* VIII, viii, 12)

MARIA CLARA BINGEMER

The question that concerns us here is primarily a matter of what constitutes the nucleus of Christianity as such, in its actual historical configuration and in its original development in the heart of late Antiquity, inheriting Judaic monotheism and structured on a cultural matrix at once polytheist and shot through with recompilations of various religions. This same concern then remains central throughout the whole history of Christianity: at the centre of medieval syntheses (debates on the One and the consistency of being) as well as at the heart of changes associated with the advent of modern times (oscillation between strict theism and pantheism). The question of monotheism still appears equally central in critiques made of Christianity today as the dominant religion of the West, faced with paradigms called post-modern, the discovery of other religious modalities, critical exploration of its own past, and so on.

Besides all this, we are also experiencing the judgment made on monotheism as being a religion of violence and exclusion and facing an apology for multiplicity, a rediscovery of cosmic or natural, not personal, dimensions. Monotheism is looking rather threatening with its concentration of power in authoritarian hands, following the pyramidal concept of 'One God in heaven, one monarch on earth' – of unhappy memory in the history of political and religious oppressions.[1]

Here I shall try to establish how Karl Rahner's theology found a way to search for an expression of the God of the Christian faith that reconciles universality and particularity, transcendence and history, economy and immanence. Then we shall see how this theology, far from inventing anything new, takes us back to the sources of the development of Christian discourse, allowing human experience to speak its faith in openness to and dialogue with the contemporary world and with other traditions.

53

I. Is Christianity a monotheism?

Among modern Christian theologians, Karl Rahner stands out for having questioned Christians of his time on the nature of the identity of their faith. Writing his observations on Augustine's *De Trinitate*, he began by posing the difficulty Christians have always faced in expressing their faith in God the Father, Son, and Holy Spirit while integrating unity and plurality: 'Despite their orthodox confession of trinitarian faith,' Christians are, in their actual lives 'hardly more than monotheists', he states.[2] On the other hand, he also points to the difficulty those who profess the Christian faith have in repeating the trinitarian formulas they were traditionally taught. Rahner calls them unintelligible for our times, accusing them of originating virtually inevitable misunderstandings.[3]

The difficulty Rahner sees with his usual clarity resides above all in the concept of 'person' used by Christian catechesis: we believe in one only God in three different persons. Rahner sees it as practically inevitable that anyone who hears this will give the word 'person' the same meaning it has in modern times, as used in other spheres of knowledge: a centre of free activity that is responsible for itself and distinguished from others by understanding and freedom.[4] Nevertheless, he stresses, it is just this aspect that has no application when we try to explain Christian teaching on the one divine nature. The Persons of the Trinity possess a unity of nature, but also of consciousness and freedom, even though this unity lives in and is determined by the mysterious tri-unity that forms the heart of the central mystery of Christianity. Although he accepted the ambiguity that such terms will never cease to show, even when Christian teaching has incorporated them in its normative definitions, Rahner was to try a daring approach to a discourse that might be able to communicate the identity of the God of Christianity to people who have passed through the sieve of Cartesian modernity.

Turning then to history as the setting for revelation, Rahner states that in it, in this limited time-span, to us human beings in our place and time, God lifts the veil covering his mystery and shows himself as he really is, in his truest and deepest identity. It is not transcendent and numinous powers representing God, or lesser forms, messengers from God, but God himself who comes to meet human beings in the history of God's self-revelation. The one who breaks the silence and speaks to human beings in human words, who walks with his creatures down the provisory roads of history, is God himself, in person, who allows himself to be experienced in himself, in the strict sense. And it is of this God revealed to all that the Old and New Testaments speak.

In the 'economy' of human life,[5] it is the very transcendent God whom no one has ever seen who reveals himself as Creator Father, who sends his Son and gives himself in him, and who lets himself be experienced as the Spirit that dwells in each one of us, presides over creation, and leads history forward. 'To the extent that in the Spirit, in the Logos-Son, and in the Father it is God himself that gives himself and not some other reality distinct from God, we should, in the strict sense, say of the Spirit, the Logos-Son, and the Father that they are the only and same God in the limitless fullness of the only divinity, in possession of one sole and same divine essence.'[6]

The hermeneutical unchangeableness and absolute difference characteristic of the God of monotheistic faith – totally other in relation to human beings – is not suppressed in trinitarian doctrine. God is still the unrealizable mystery, holy and eternal, the foundation of the transcendental existence of human beings. Nevertheless, as Rahner says in a fine recovery of the source of Christian revelation, '. . . he is not only the God of infinite distance but also seeks to be the God of absolute proximity in true self-communication, and in this way God is present in the spiritual depths of our existence, as well as in the actuality of our history in space and time.'[7]

II. The Trinity: mystery of salvation

In his trinitarian theology, Rahner is then concerned to show that the Trinity is not a logical mystery but a mystery of salvation for humankind. So we always have to think of it starting from the economic level (God acting in our favour and for us) and moving to the immanent (God in God's eternal life of perfect communion). In doing so, Rahner is simply, with faithful creativity, following the Church's richest tradition, notably that which was developed in the early centuries of Christianity by the Fathers.[8] Intimately and harmoniously, he brings together two categories that have always formed the basic binomial of Christianity: divine transcendence and human history. What is on high, the divine life, the mystery of God, is definitively brought down, to the level of human life and history. This is the major mystery the first Christian communities perceived and experienced in their living together with Jesus of Nazareth, confirmed by his resurrection. Jesus' faith in the *Abba* who was none other than the God of Abraham, Joseph, and Jacob developed into faith in Jesus himself, recognized as the Son of God. The absence of the Galilean through his death on the cross gave way to the joy of experiencing him living and witnessed in the community through means of his Spirit.[9]

The faith of those men and women introduced an unbreakable bond between heaven and earth. The eternal and absolute God gives history existence and consistence, in which salvation is offered and comes about, in the form of a fullness of love that re-creates humanity from within and leads to its end, which is at the same time its foundation. The eternal Trinity is the Alpha and Omega of history, love in perfect communion. Such thinking brought the mystery of the God whom no one has ever seen to the level of earth, in the midst of human relationships with their ambiguity and simultaneous content of sin and grace. And in doing so it showed that human history is the setting *par excellence* in which the Creator lovingly proffers salvation to his creatures, while they are still lost and incapable of putting themselves on the way through their own efforts.

It is in this unheard-of proximity, in which Love makes itself known in the midst of non-love and conflict, that human beings can still make the experience of the God who is love. The One God who is revealed as the Father of Jesus offers love and desires to be loved. This God had already, in his revelation to the people of Israel, proposed love of him as an imperative and a commandment: 'You shall love the Lord your God with all your heart, and with all your soul, and with all your might'.[10]

Rahner would say, then, that what enables us to believe in a One and Triune God as fullness of Love is the fact he manifests himself thus, in this manner, in history. Not as a phenomenon that leaves the enigma of existence untouched, but as the gift of his own trinitarian presence and the possibility of access to this.[11] Israel, without ceasing for a moment to be the people of the Law, is the people of love. And it was this love that was to shape its identity as a people, its journey, and its self-realization. Nevertheless, the whole experience of loving and being loved that characterized the journey of the chosen people, as well as the ineluctable and exclusive demands of that love, from very early on proved not only affective and accessible to the senses. It had a very concrete and real dimension, this love of God who was to require, as a proof of faithfulness to his person, the working of justice and right for all, but especially for those most deprived of strength, of a voice, of privileges: orphans, the poor, widows, foreigners. . . .[12]

The revelation of God as love itself is nevertheless shown in God's love for us. This means, according to Rahner, that 'God acts in relation to justified men [and women] as Father, Word, and Spirit and is at the same time this in himself and for himself'.[13] This divine identity and this imperative of being loved above all things rises and shines as a primordial demand in the face of others, of neighbours, for whose sake we must practise the love freely given to us. And it shines in a paradigmatic form in the face of Jesus of Nazareth, in whom the Christian community recognizes the Son of God and God himself.

It will be Jesus, therefore, who, according to Rahner, opens for once and all, in history, access to the presence and love of the Trinity. It is in this man, 'who invoked and named God as his Father (Abba) and who, through his actions and his teaching, but above all in the way he faced up to violence and even death, and in his resurrection from among the dead, showed there was a link between the Father and himself', that we can find access to the mystery of the Trinity. For Rahner, therefore, it is in the narrative of the human life of Jesus, accepted as Lord, through the 'new birth' made possible by the Holy Spirit,[14] that the trinitarian horizon becomes entwined with theological discourse, in mutual fertilization and reciprocal enlightenment.[15]

The incarnation of the Son of God was to show that God is not just an Idea or the One or the Beginning of the philosophers, but a living being: a God who came to talk to human beings, to reveal himself to them, loving and desiring to be loved. If the Christ Jesus is accepted as the Word,[16] or as the perfect expression and mirror of the Father's glory,[17] this is because in God there exists not just an absolute and rigid oneness but also a difference that allows God to be 'outside himself', to communicate himself in the midst of what is not God, 'altering' his divinity without losing it, and coming to take on the history of the human race. This is then Rahner's fundamental axiom, a milestone in the development of contemporary trinitarian theology: 'The Trinity that shows itself in the economy of salvation is the immanent Trinity, and vice-versa.'[18]

With this axiom, Rahner introduced several breaks into the treatise on the Trinity. The first of these is in the conception of trinitarian theology as two separate treatises. The more traditional theological schools, especially that of the neo-scholastics, had the greatest difficulty in seeing that the Trinity is above all the manifestation of God in the history of salvation. The whole theological edifice of this theology starts from above, upholding an unbridgeable hermeneutical abyss between economy and eternity. Rahner, posits, on the contrary, that God himself has bridged this abyss, through the *kenosis* of the Son, who descended to the ultimate depths of human humiliation and suffering, before then being raised to the glory of the Father.[19] The logic of the Trinity conceived purely on the basis of its immanence could not allow for its connection to the humble and patient history of salvation, which comes about among the fidelities and infidelities of human beings, and also to certain of Jesus' statements in the Gospels, about no one knowing the day or the hour, 'neither the angels in heaven, nor the Son, but only the Father'.[20]

By daring to take a step farther with his axiom concerning the most classical conception of trinitarian theology, Rahner is not opposing the starting points from above and from below. He is simply establishing the intimate link between God and creation, between the divine and history, between the transcendent and the earthly. And this link is the gift of Truth and Love to human beings; God becomes the closest intimate of his creatures in their joys and sorrows. This is verified in Jesus Christ, who is the exemplar *par excellence* of the economic Trinity being the immanent Trinity and vice-versa. Jesus Christ is not the incarnation of the God of the philosophers and theists. He is the Word, the Word of the God who spoke his name and showed his face in the history of a people, leading it from captivity to freedom. And because, in the Trinity, the Word is the self-expression of the Father, at once intimately bound to him and different from him, he can be the true face of the Father on earth, taking on human existence and freedom as his own.[21]

III. Christianity: religion or way?

Christian theology today is coming more and more decidedly to see the identity of Christianity not as a religion but as a way and a proposal for life.[22] The God who reveals himself in the heart of the history of Israel, fulfilling his promises in Jesus of Nazareth, is the God of Abraham, Isaac, and Jacob, and none other. At its centre, therefore, Christian faith has a person and not a religion properly so-called. The Christian event starts and happens in the world in the flesh and the face of Jesus of Nazareth, who in Galilee began to proclaim that the Kingdom of God had already arrived.

In many aspects the New Testament shows Jesus as a religious man: a pious Jew, a man of faith, an Israelite. He frequented the synagogue, read and knew the Torah. In other ways, however, it presents him as having a very free and somewhat revolutionary approach to the expressions of his faith: he distances himself from his own religious traditions and, when rejected by his religious community, does not institute a new form of worship or leave his disciples any ritual or legal code or written creed that might have provided them with a precise religious guide.[23] Still less does he proclaim any God other than the God of Israel.

His preaching is, on the contrary, aimed at a future open to the proclamation of a good news, that of the Kingdom of God, which is coming, which is already here, at hand, and which has to be welcomed in faith. The faith he proposes is trust in him as the way that leads to God, and which has to be followed radically, breaking or relativizing all other bonds, whether of family, profession, or even religion. The faith born of his person, his life, death, and resurrection, and which will be called Christian faith, will come to understand itself as a gift, gratuitous and unforeseen, received from the Spirit of God and not from any human legacy, even that of a religion. This is an inspiration that flows from the beginning and for ever and will therefore become the key to re-reading history and the scriptures, all the while providing liberation from any religious legacy, so that human beings, putting aside the justice that comes from cultic worship and the law, can present themselves before God in a posture of thanksgiving, stripped and humble, placing their trust solely in the life and death of Jesus from love, in his raising by the Father who upholds his way, and by the faith he inspires and arouses.[24]

This is why the Christian faith is defined not by ritual gestures or doctrinal confession, however important these may be. Christianity has no permanent guarantee but is, on the contrary, always open to being projected beyond itself. Based on the 'Magna Carta' of the Sermon on the Mount, which declares the poor, the meek, the merciful, and the peaceful blessed, the Way set out by Jesus can only understand itself on the basis of the unbreakable bond between God and one's neighbour. And so it constantly recalls that the God of Israel is the God of love, who loves and wants to be loved, and who seeks above all that this love be poured out especially on those who lack or are denied love in this world.

What prescriptions, then, does the way of life inaugurated by Jesus called the Christ entail? Simply the charity that serves the poor, forgives our enemy, gives a cup of water to a stranger – and, in the stranger, in those who suffer any kind of injustice, Christian faith finds its Lord and its God, far more than in rites and doctrinal codes. And so it cannot be confined to temples and sacred spaces, because it is never totally possessed but is always on the way, having to receive itself constantly and directly from the Spirit of God. In this sense, it transcends the religion that is its support and the vehicle for its expression and transmission.[25] Its true form of expression is the deepest and most human things that human beings do.

In professing their faith, Christians have from the start understood themselves as believers in one sole God. The Nicene-Constantinopolitan profession of faith starts by saying very clearly, 'I believe in one God, creator of heaven and earth, and of all that is, seen and unseen'. What is there, in this first article of faith, that could set Christians apart from their Jewish and Muslim brothers and sisters? In my view: nothing.

Even when we move on to the second article of the creed, in which the Oneness of God opens out into the difference of Jesus Christ, only-begotten Son, Our Lord, there should not be difference *and* estrangement. Difference, certainly, but a difference that seeks to draw close. By proclaiming belief in Jesus Christ, the Christian faith is proclaiming its desire to make its own the faith of this Jesus, who continually called this God whom no one has ever seen Father and established a relationship of deep love and complete availability with him. This faith is at the same time stating that it understands the human condition as being constantly open to relationship with others, in a perpetual and growing openness to the practice of love and justice to all, above all to the weakest and most vulnerable, as Jesus of Nazareth showed. And finally, by proclaiming its belief in the Holy Spirit, it is saying it believes that God himself is not just above humankind, or walking at our side through history; God also dwells within us, enabling us to enjoy the ineffable experience of communion in love.

Trinitarian monotheism tells us that we are children not of loneliness but of communion. And therefore, just through the relationship that produces communion, even if imperfect and incomplete, the human condition fulfils itself and transcends itself, taking its place in the whole of creation. This way of universal life is offered to the whole human race, not just to Christians of any denomination or all of them. Without denying faith in a single God, Christianity opens a space in which differences can be welcomed and integrated through practising the love God revealed in human history, in the story of Jesus the Galilean and in every personal story in which he lives through his Spirit. By experiencing love and giving love we find the gate open to the one and true God who is revealed as Father, Son, and Holy Spirit and is love in himself and for us.

Conclusion: If you see the Trinity you see love

The course we have been following here, under the guidance of Karl Rahner, a great theologian of the twentieth century, takes us back to the fourth century, to another great theologian, Augustine of Hippo.

The kernel of Christian revelation of God is love, as stated in the First Letter of John, which Augustine comments on in chapter VIII of his treatise *De Trinitate*. The fact that God is love, communication, outpouring of life, radically alters the understanding we can have of God, of ourselves, and of the world. The Triune God displays a model of how oneness and multiplicity do and should relate to one another. The trinitarian Unity is not either a reified oneness or a collective uniformity. It is not the narcissistic passion of the solitary ego or tyrannical oppression by the plurality for the benefit of its own monadic ego. It is precisely a network of relationships, an interchange of life.[26]

Relationship – being in relationship, interaction and interlocution with others – forms the deepest essence of reality. The supreme and true reality, both in the sphere of creatures and that of divinity, is 'being with others' and 'being for others'.[27] Only on this basis can we attain true unity, which is not a closed unity but an open one, in communion. A powerful indicator is undoubtedly the fact that Augustine, at the heart of his *De Trinitate*, after having tried to explain the mystery of the Trinity through his exegesis of biblical theophanies and attempted to make the notions of substance and relationship converge in the notion of person, should finally point to love, charity, as the privileged way of access to the reality that has always been most invisible and inaccessible to human thought: the identity of the one God in three persons.

Translated by Paul Burns

Notes

1. See the critique of monotheism as concentration of power made by Leonardo Boff in his *A Trindade e a Sociedade* (Eng. trans. *Trinity and Society*, Tunbridge Wells and Maryknoll, NY: Burns & Oates and Orbis Books, [2]1992, esp. pp. 20–3).

2. Cf. K. Rahner, 'Dieu Trinité, fondement transcendant de l'histoire du salut', in *Mysterium Salutis*, vol. 6, Paris: Cerf, 1970, pp. 13–140. (Fr. trans. of 'Der dreifaltige Gott als transzendenter Urgrund der Heilsgeschichte', in J. Donceel (ed.), *Der Heilsgeschichte vor Christus*; Eng. trans. *The Trinity*, New York: Herder & Herder, 1997.)

3. Rahner, *Grundkurs des Glaubens*, Freiburg: Herder, [11]2005 (Eng. trans. *Foundations of Christian Belief*, New York: Herder & Herder, 1997.) Here Port. trans., 1989, p. 166: 'With all due respect to the official formulae of the Magisterium and to the classical expressions of the Christian doctrine of the Trinity, and taking for granted the acceptance in faith of what these formulae mean, we nevertheless have to admit that statements referring to the Trinity on the level of its catechetical formulations are virtually unintelligible for people today and cannot fail to produce almost inevitable equivocations.'

4. *Ibid.*, p. 167.

5. 'Economy' comes from the Greek *oikonomía*, meaning administration, ordering of a house, organization, distribution, economy'; *via* the Latin *oeconomìa*, disposition, order, arrangement, economy (of a poem or speech).

6. Rahner, *Foundations*, here Port. pp. 168–9.

7. *Ibid.*, p. 170.

8. Cf. for example St Irenaeus of Lyon's phrase: 'The Perfect Man, the Son of the Father, made all things new by bringing himself,' in *Adv. Haer.*, 4.34, 1. This contains all the themes dear to Irenaeus: the making new and recapitulation of all things in Christ, as well as God's pedagogy in his revelation, which reaches its highest point in the incarnation of the Word. See also the fine article by A. Pimentel, 'A atualidade de uma questão a doutrina da união hipostática em Cirilio de Alexandria e Karl Rahner', *Perspectiva Teológica* 35 (2003), 325–40.

9. The Fathers took the same view. Pimentel, *art. cit.* above, quotes Cyril of Alexandria's fine words on the hypostatic union in his second letter to Nestorius: 'Two different natures meet in one true unity, but from the two [comes] one sole Christ and Son; the difference of the natures was not suppressed by the union; on the contrary, his divinity and his humanity form for us a single Lord and Son and Christ, through their indivisible and ineffable meeting in unity.' Cf. P.-T. Camelot, *Ephèse et Chalcedoine*, Paris: Ed. de l'Orante, p. 192.

10. Deut. 6.5; cf. 11.1.

11. Cf. Y. Tourenne in his Introduction to Rahner's 'Dieu Trinité', *art. cit.*, n. 2 above.

12. Cf. Deut. 10.18; 16.11; 24.17.

13. Cf. Rahner's 'God in the New Testament', in *Theological Investigations*, vol. 1, a study he also cites in 'Dieu Trinité'.

14. Cf. John 3.3.

15. Rahner, quoted Tourenne, *art. cit.*, pp. v–vi.

16. Cf. John 1.1.

17. Heb. 1.1–3.

18. Rahner, 'Dieu Trinité', p. 29.

19. Cf. Phil. 2.8–9; Eph. 4.9–10.

20. Cf. Mark 13.32; John 14.28; Acts 1.10ff.

21. Cf. John 14.9; see also 'Dieu Trinité'. p. 40.

22. Cf. J. Comblin, *O Caminho. Ensaio sobre o seguimento de Jesus*, São Paulo: Paulus, ²2005; J. Moingt, *Dieu qui vient à l'homme. Du deuil au dévoilement de Dieu*, vol. 1, Paris: Cerf, 2002, p, 84.

23. Moingt, *op. cit.*, p. 84.

24. *Ibid.*, pp. 84–5.

25. *Ibid.*, p. 85.

26. Cf. what some contemporary theologians have said on this aspect, such as G. Greschake, *An der drei-einen Gott glaubens: ein Schlüssel zum Vesrstehen*, Freiburg: Herder, 1998; *idem, Der dreieine Gott: eine trinitarische Theologie*,

Freiburg: Herder, [5]2007; L. Boff, *Trinity and Society*, *op. cit.*; J. Moltmann, *The Trinity and the Kingdom of God*, London and San Francisco: SCM Press and Harper & Row, 1981, among others.

27. Greshake, *An der drei-einen Gott glauben*, *op. cit.* (here Sp. trans., 2002, p. 32).

Part Two: Ways of Thinking God's Unity within the Christian Traditions

Monotheism and Violence versus Monotheism and Universal Brother-/Sisterhood

Subjects that date from the distant past, especially if they involve ethical or religious contents, gather up theoretical pre-judgments and emotional baggage. They reach our current consideration already over-determined, with the result that our primary concerns have to be a scrupulous effort to seek clarity of concept and emotive serenity. Only in this way can we avoid both aggressive hyper-criticality and apologetic hyper-defensiveness.

This general observation has a very special application to relations between violence and religion. In fact, it can often happen that a sort of theoretical violence infects even our dealing with actual violence. Distinguishing levels of discourse and self-criticism then becomes the condition for a dialogic collaboration that seeks to understand others and, in the final analysis, make use of their critique in building a genuine self-understanding of ourselves.

This is what I shall at least attempt here, distinguishing first the different levels of discourse and then trying to define the 'essence' of what Christian monotheism is – or should be – before finally insisting on the need for collaboration among religions.

I. External critiques of monotheism and violence

Since the Enlightenment revolution, religion has become one of the focal points for critique of the past. Ecclesiastical forms of resistance to many aspects of the process of emancipation, and above all the Inquisition and the horrifying memory of the wars of religion, turned Christianity – and the monotheistic aspect of it – into the target of harsh accusations of being a fomenter of violence. Recourse to the 'noble savage' (even if many of them were known to be cannibals) and to foreign cultures (Chinese, Persian . . .) were indirect – and idealized – recourses for presenting alternative visions of a peaceable humankind.[1] Hume expressed this clearly: 'The intolerance of almost all religions that uphold the oneness of God is as notable as the opposite principle of the polytheists. The irreconcilable and narrow spirit of the Jews is well known.'² In the last sixty years the accusation has become direct and more explicit, showing a neo-pagan, post-modern, and Nietzschean tendency to 'praise of polytheism' (Marquard). Lately, Jan Assmann has put ancient Egypt forward as an alternative of pacifying monotheism.

In the persistence and detail of his approach, Assmann – and one has to be grateful for his balanced clarifications³ – makes clear something that is not always duly brought out: the *external nature* common to this type of consideration. From an alien environment and using conceptual tools unsuited to actual religious intentionality, this produces a whole conceptual construct without seeking sufficient *Einfühlung* and – at least at first – with an excessively polemical approach. Together with this goes another very common characteristic: idealizing the religion taken as a contrast, while concentrating on the defects and abuses of the one criticized.

Pagan polytheism is thus turned into an appreciation of the vitality and sacredness of the universe, pluralist and tolerant, enthusiastic and festive, welcoming and in no way fanatical, non-violent and respectful of differences.⁴ In its turn, Egyptian 'cosmotheism', unlike the monotheism of the 'Mosaic distinction', represents the complete reconciliation between gods and world, divinity and politics; it is accepting and patient by nature; it even includes a moral optimism, devoid of guilt or sin, which belong only to Christian monotheism.

No matter that in order for the neo-pagan construct to function, one needs to ignore all the bloody struggles and rivalries among the Homeric gods, to forget the critiques of the pre-Socratics or of Plato, not to mention the persecutions carried out by pagan religions. No matter either that if we are to idealize cosmotheism we have to make a 'mnemohistorical' reinterpretation of the violence with which Akhenaten, in introducing a single God, destroyed temples, removed other gods, and killed priests, as indeed of the bloody response, once he was dead, to restore the old religion. In this way one can jump almost two centuries of actual history – imitating Freud in this sort of re-editing of his theories – in order to make Moses 'mnemohistorically' contemporary with Akhenaten, and five or six in order to make him into a monotheist.⁵

Monotheism, on the other hand, is made into the counter-figure that subsumes all the evils of intolerance, violence, negation of difference, and elimination of its opposite. Neither the Decalogue, nor denunciation by the prophets, nor 'judge not' and love of enemies, nor 'be merciful', nor the cross, nor the charitable activity of Francis of Assisi (alongside abuses and inquisitors) count for anything in this interpretation of history and religious judgment. A one-sided hyper-critique of this sort– which can sometimes become maddening – is characteristic of a typically Western negativity with regard to tradition, particularly religious tradition. This hyper-critique needs to be named for what it is, precisely for the sake of a realistic dialogue.

Once we have named it, however, we also need to recognize its truth – even, with a degree of theological humour, to accept it as a penance for all our historical sins. Above all, we should avoid any temptation to apologetics. We should make use of criticism as revealing of serious deviations and terrible abuses, which are real and demand our attention. Basically, the harshness of the protest also implies a positive recognition: the faults matter so much because they contrast with religion's true essence. 'All too often, we believers have betrayed the high ideals that we ourselves have preached.'[6]

II. Internal criticism of monotheism and violence

The ambivalence of the religious spirit is obvious: it is capable of arousing the greatest heroism and of fostering the cruellest contradictions. In various ways and with its particular dangers, it affects all religions, be they mystical, prophetic, or wisdom, though each demonstrates its specific potentialities and proclivities, both for promoting peace or fomenting violence.[7] Here we should focus on the Bible and not close our eyes to its tremendous realism. Speaking of *general* violence, Raymund Schwager states: 'No other human activity or experience is mentioned as frequently, either in the world of work and the economy, or in that of family and sexuality, or in that that of nature or science.'[8] The astonishing thing is that it implicates even *God*: 'The theme of bloody vengeance wreaked by God is found even more often in the Old Testament than the problem of human violence. Around *one thousand* passages speak of Yahweh's anger being aroused, of his punishing with death or ruination, judging like a consuming fire, avenging himself and threatening annihilation. [. . .] No other subject appears as frequently as the bloodthirsty actions of God.'[9]

References could be multiplied,[10] but those indicated suffice to show the deadly seriousness of the problem: 'The image of God as warrior constitutes the real scandal of the Old Testament for modern man, including the Christian.'[11] And Giuseppe Barbaglio pushes the point: 'The question becomes literally anguishing when God himself commands violent actions that are so many expressions of obedience to his will', such as 'holy war' and expressions in some of the Psalms.[12]

All this would not be so bad if it could be shut away in the remote past, since historical consciousness teaches us to be understanding of phenomena that can appear shocking *today*. The real problem is its *anachronistic persistence*. The mental habits of biblical literalism, together with pressure from the cultural environment, prevented people from drawing the true consequences of the God proclaimed as love. Mental intransigence took over, and when this was allied with power, so did persecution, war, and slaughter. On this point Origen himself did not always live up to Celsus, and Augustine continually hardened his position, until he justified the persecution of heretics:[13] his *compelle intrare* was to have a tragic influence on later history,[14] including St Thomas Aquinas.[15]

Feeling for history and biblical criticism need to combine to bring about a radical cleansing of the Christian imaginary. Avoiding subterfuges and false emollients, we have to recognize that such horrors are real if we are to be able to show honestly that they stem from mistaken interpretations: God – the real one, not the one of our human projections – *never* ordered deaths, exterminations, or plagues. These are *errors*-on-the-journey, understandable *at the time* and perhaps not blameworthy, which might even have advanced revelation; *today*, however, they cannot be upheld without sinning through critical ignorance and moral irresponsibility. It is not good enough to say with St Augustine that 'the Church persecutes through charity; unbelievers through cruelty' (*Letter* 185, 11), or with A. Michel, quoting a French archbishop: 'The Church has the intransigence of truth and of charity'.[16] Nor should we fall back on obviously obfuscating explanations: 'Violent, our God? Yes, but in a good way!'[17]

These quotes are not an ill-intentioned diversion but a warning to take very seriously the fact that an improper use of the Bible – even with 'scientific' apparatus – still fosters violent phantasms. We should not, for example, go on *praying*[18] psalms laden with hatred and vengeance, on the pretext that they are speaking of the devil. Nor should we 'theologize' God's 'anger', justifying it on the grounds that 'God is living and not apathetic', 'good but also just', or that salvation is not 'cheap grace' – misinterpreting grace as though it were dear and measured, rather than, more gloriously, *a free gift*.[19]

We can never be too careful or too punctilious on this supremely sensitive point, since our deepest image of God decisively affects religious experience and behaviour: *a violent God in the end engenders violent faithful*. Contrary to a particular theological rhetoric, we have to insist on the need to revise certain 'traditional' ideas that are venerable only in appearance but really relics of fundamentalist readings, and which are *now* doing a great deal of damage. We cannot go on stating, even if theologians of the stature of Barth, Bultmann, and Moltmann do, that Jesus 'on the cross took upon himself and suffered God's wrath' or that this 'shows what God's anger with the whole world really is'.

I am convinced that it is not even permissible to stay with the definition – originating with St Augustine and popularized by Rudolf Otto[20] – of God as *fascinans et tremendum* mystery. Otto himself has tended to soften this, but it has to be abandoned *tout court*, at least if we are to take the *Abba* proclaimed by Jesus seriously, as unqualified 'love' (1 John 4.8, 16) and Father who does not condemn the prodigal son; who is *only* grace, forgiveness, and salvation for the good *and* the evil (Matt. 5.45); who, forgiving unconditionally, seeks to cast out all 'fear' (1 John 4.18).

The concepts that it is vital to revise in this sense are multiple and very central: the evil in the world as *punishment* for an original sin, a literal interpretation of the sacrifice of *Isaac*,[21] a vision of hell as eternal suffering that serves to increase the joy of the blessed. . . . If we do not interpret these from inside with a critical faith, they will come back from outside as unanswerable accusations against the faith. Here, indeed, the expression 'canonical exegesis' has a precise and almost tautological application: the truth of the Bible lies in its entirety, because revelation is definitive only at the end of its course. So we need to read the Bible *backwards*, judging and ordering it as a whole from the God revealed in Jesus: 'Love your enemies, do good to those who hate you, bless those who curse you, pray for those who abuse you. . . . Be merciful, just as your Father is merciful' (Luke 7.27–8, 36; cf. Matt. 5.44–8).

III. Use, abuse, and dangerous affinities

A proper hermeneutics and of course the resulting theology should state clearly and fearlessly that any violence in God's name is *abuse* and distortion, special pleading in the name of particular interests, be they economic, political, military. . . . Freud put it with bitter harshness: 'Judging by our unconscious desires and inclinations, we are no more than a band of criminals, just like our early ancestors'.[22] This dark background also holds the root that can poison religion too. The Pope recalled this in Palestine, one of the most violent places on earth – and most manipulated by apparently religious motivations.

What is obvious is that such a serious, repeated, and persistent abuse alerts us to the existence of an undeniable affinity or proclivity. Our special pleading would be impossible without this inner complicity that nests in the most recondite corners of religious experience. Religion in general and monotheism in particular have all too easily contributed to stimulating violence and justifying wars. Their potential for *absolutization*, which constitutes their greatness, makes us capable of maximum generosity and renunciation, to the point of laying down our own life. But, wrongly orientated, it leads to total devaluation and absolute violence. Ricoeur spoke of a horizontal overflowing of vertical transcendence,[23] and later clarified: 'The summit of violence coincides with the summit of hope, when the latter claims to totalize meaning.'[24] The most horrible manifestation comes about when, in the name of the God-love, we kill individuals and exterminate peoples.

Religious complicity is born above all from alliance with power, theoretical and/or institutional. To counter this, the Churches urgently need to find the right balance between the divine absolute and the human relative. This will not prove easy: *relativism* infects the divine absolute with the human, undermining ideals and meaning; *authoritarianism* infects human mediation with the absolute, excluding and destroying difference.[25]

The latter situation marks especially the 'Catholic' danger: an ecclesiastical *power* unmediated by its inclusion as service in the community (LG, Ch. II)) generates an anti-evangelical style of internal violence. Fortunately, these no longer leads to the pyres of the Inquisition, but the fact that Häring preferred a Nazi tribunal to certain curial proceedings, and that Congar was driven to the verge of suicide, ring alarm bells. Only a Church that is fraternal in its proceedings and humble in truth can really make the truth of the God of Peace visible.

IV. Universal brother-/sisterhood as the truth of monotheism

Not fearing self-criticism also gives us grounds for stating that, despite its terrible historical contradictions, violence in monotheism is *an abuse contrary to its essence*. This is where the true criterion lies. Husserl did not contain his enthusiasm for Otto's *Das Heilige*, but he pointed to two important requirements: (1) 'separation between occasional action and *eidos*'; and (2) 'an essential typological organization of the strata of religious facts in their necessary and essential development'.[26] This means repeating the original genesis in order to reach the essence through historical variations and on this basis distinguishing the genuine from the spurious.

A detailed consideration of this is not possible here. But it is worth pointing out that monotheism, in its *eidos*, represents a positive achievement by the religious spirit. This is shown by its appearance in the axial age, replacing tribalist and particularist spirits by a universal human one. It is confirmed by religious studies, with the Vienna School affirming its affinity with the primary figure of the Supreme Being and with Pettazzoni defining the reflexive and late nature of strict monotheism. Philosophy has understood it since the pre-Socratics. In my view, only an 'anti-monotheist affect' can turn us back beyond this philosophical acquisition: the Divine could not be discovered as the transcendent foundation of the world, but once it is discovered, the speculative legitimacy of its unitary nature becomes hard to question (remember that authors such as Walter Otto see 'monotheism' even behind Greek polytheism).[27]

It seems equally hard to question that a 'typological stratification' shows the monotheist affirmation – one God *of all and for all* – as forming the best basis for universal brother-/sisterhood. There could be a polytheism that allows for difference in peace, but human realism and indeed literature cannot hide its (greater) proclivity to discord and struggle. Henotheism – 'I have my god; the rest have theirs' – may appear more conciliatory, but in reality, especially political reality, it tends to impose itself by force: the horrific struggles among the gods of the *Enuma Elish* (Babylonian creation myth) well reflect the armed domination of Marduk, Babylon's 'own' god. And it is symptomatic that when Jan Assmann wants to accentuate the intransigence of the 'Mosaic distinction', he defines as 'political monotheism' what he himself recognizes as henotheism: 'the existence of other gods is here completely accepted'.[28]

Here, however, it is worth pointing to two facts that show anti-violence to be intrinsic to monotheism. The first, the *paternal symbol*, so central in Christianity, shows this intuitively: it can be misinterpreted, but *in itself* it indicates that it is impossible to *believe* in a God-Father without loving the other-brother, even the violent brother: 'Love your enemies, do good to those who hate you' (Luke 6.27).[29]

The second is a historical confirmation that proves particularly enlightening for being placed just at the beginning of biblical monotheism. Given Israel's precarious position in Palestine after the Babylonian exile, subject to the empire and surrounded by enemies, its *temptation* was to violence, making the God recently discovered to be the only one its own. The reforms of Nehemiah proceeded in this direction, forbidding marriage with foreigners and even dissolving existing ones, concentrating on the Temple, the Law,

and the Sabbath, thereby excluding all others from salvation. But someone understood that this was constitutively wrong. Concealing his name
– because he was risking his life by transgressing both the unwritten civil
code and 'official teaching'[30] – he composed a theological novella to defend
the true meaning of monotheism. 'Jonah' had to learn, against all distortions,
that God, because God is *unique* and *God of all*, wishes to save all: 'But this
was very displeasing to Jonah, and he became angry. He prayed to the Lord
and said, "O Lord! Is not this what I said while I was still in my own country? That is why I fled to Tarshish at the beginning; for I knew that you are
a gracious God and merciful, slow to anger and abounding in steadfast love,
and ready to relent from punishing"' (Jon. 4.1–2).

V. Monotheism and dialogue

It is not only power that contaminates; so does an abstract vision of *truth*,
which tends toward dogmatism and the *extra ecclesiam* . . . . Juan Luis
Segundo contrasted the *digital* truth of yes/no, all/nothing with what he
called an *iconic* or analogical truth of progressive and plural approximation:
less/more, good/better.[31] In 2 + 2, only 4 can be the truth, but any Tom,
Dick or Mary can be *truly* 'my friends', even if in different ways. Assmann
and others take for granted that the truth of monotheism necessarily creates
the *excluding* distinction true/false, good/bad, all/nothing, as if relationship
to the divine mystery had to be digitally univocal and not, on the contrary, a
plural and asymptotic approximation.

Personally, I always start from the principle, 'all religions are true', in that
they are discovery and acceptance of the divine mystery. Hence the truth of
pluralism, even if human finitude inevitably changes it into 'asymmetric pluralism'. There is certainly no room for an 'anything goes', since not everything is equal in religions. This, however, does not mean *exclusivism* but a
realist appreciation of the limits, first of one's own religion, *semper reformanda*
(from the warrior Yahweh to Jesus' Abba), and then of the others (from magic
or human sacrifice to the disinterested love of the Sufis or Hindu *bhakti*).[32]

Monotheism, showing religions drawn by the *same* Mystery that seeks
to give itself to *all of them* and that *none of them* can embrace, 'essentially'
calls them to dialogue and cooperation, seeking a less imperfect truth: 'you
received without payment; give without payment' (Matt. 10.8). This is not
to deny the legitimacy of recognizing the definitive in history, something
that I, as a Christian, confess in Jesus Christ. But the *historical-actual way*
we receive the definitive does not entail all-round perfection, or absence in

others, or exclusive appropriation. Denying others means impoverishing oneself, and egoistical appropriation means contradicting God. Every religion has something to give and something to receive: actual religious truth is an ever-unfinished symphony, as Duquoc and Baltasar state.

This applies to the monotheisms, which deny their own essence by competing with one another instead of collaborating by bringing and receiving the best of each: 'If Israel is rooted in hope and Christianity devoted to charity, Islam is focused on faith.'[33] Here, it can prove very difficult to extract controlled meaning from trinitarian *speculations* (to the point of Augustine's 'We speak so as not remain silent'), which can divide more than unite. It is better to speak in a concrete and not exclusivist way of their *deep truth*: of the *filial* relationship shown so intensely in the life and teaching of Christ, common for all in his humanity, definitive for Christians, but also a brother for Judaism and a prophet for Islam; of the primordial paternal *Mystery* to which all refer, perhaps in special dialogue with Eastern traditions; and of the *Spirit* that creates and inspires all reality, accepting and transforming the sacrality both of the world religions and of the various natural religions.

Christians, however, find mainly in the cross of Christ – as a continual lesson to them, never adequately assimilated, and a maieutic offer to others – both the 'scandal' and 'madness' of all violence and the unimaginable glory of non-violence revealed with the greatest force and clarity. Even the cross can be instrumentalized, but, as the best of Girard shows, *in its truth* it provides the most effective unmasking of the two great deceits: the 'mimetic violence' that uses God to justify the various 'crusades' against rivals and dissidents, and recourse to 'scapegoats', which sacrifices poor, marginal, and defenceless peoples, groups, and individuals on the altar of progress. Jesus provides this without violence or vengeance: 'Put your sword back into its sheath', and without legitimizing ideological justifications: 'If I have spoken rightly, why do you strike me?'. His inspirational power, which has never vanished from history and could inspire both Gandhi and Martin Luther King, shows the religious transversality of his truth.

This transversality summons us to the exciting and never-ending task of uniting all religions so that they can overcome their theoretical differences and collaborate in what is decisive and certainly more achievable: seeking, as Hans Küng has famously insisted on, union in the exercise of love, putting an end to all types of violence and intolerance among themselves and cooperating with all humanizing efforts at instilling peace among nations.

Translated by Paul Burns

Notes

1. Cf. P. Hazard, *La crise de la conscience européenne, 1680–1715*, Paris, 1935.
2. D. Hume, *The Natural History of Religion, IX*, in A. Flew (ed.), *David Hume. Writings on Religion*, La Salle, Il, 1992, pp. 146–7.
3. I am referring to *Die Mosaische Unterscheidung oder der Preis des Monotheismus* (Munich, 2003), which clarifies his *Moses the Egyptian: The Memory of Egypt in Western Monotheism* (Cambridge, Mass.: Harvard U.P., 1997).
4. I am taking almost word for word the characterization by C. Duquoc, 'Monotheism and Unitary Ideology', *Concilium* 177 (1985/1), 59–66. The whole of this excellent monograph remains worth reading.
5. Cf. also J. A. Zamora, 'Monoteísmo, intolerancia y violencia. El debate teológico-político sobre la "distinción mosaica"', in R. Mate and J. A. Zamora (eds), *Nuevas Teologías Políticas*, Barcelona, 2006, pp. 197–207; R. Gibellini in this issue, below, pp. 113–18.
6. UNESCO 1994, in F. Toradeflot (ed.), *Diálogo entre religiones. Textos fundamentales*, Madrid, 2002, p. 47.
7. Cf. M. C. Bingemer (ed.), *Violência e Religião*, São Paulo, 2001; X. Pikaza, *Violencia y diálogo de religiones*, Santander, 2004.
8. R. Schwager, *Brauchen wir einen Sündenbock?*, Munich, 1978, p. 58.
9. *Ibid.*, pp. 65–6.
10. Cf., *e.g.*, G. Barbaglio, *Dios ¿violento?*, Estella, 1992, containing a wealth of information.
11. D. Miller, 'God the Warrior: A Problem in Biblical Interpretation and Apologetics', *Interpretation* 19 (1965), 40.
12. *Op. cit.*, 11.
13. Cf. A. Fürst, 'Monotheismus und Gewalt. Fragen an der Früzheit des Christentums', *Stimmen der Zeit* 154 (2004), 521–31.
14. Cf. O. Karrer, 'Compelle intrare', LThK 3 (1959), 27–8.
15. '. . . if money forgers and other wrongdoers are quickly and justly put to death by secular princes, the more so can heretics, from the moment they are convicted of heresy, be not only excommunicated, but also justly executed' (2/2, q.11, a.3 c).
16. 'Tolérance', in DTC 15 (1946), 1222.
17. M. Girard (not René!), 'La violence de Dieu dans la Bible juive', *Science et Esprit* 39 (1987), 69; quoted by Barbaglio, *op.cit.*, p. 10.
18. Studying the Psalms and trying to learn from them as stages on the journey to 'Christian difference' is another matter.
19. This expression can be conflated with other motives, seriously obscuring the gratuity of grace. See, *e.g.*, what a theologian as brilliant and committed to *sola fides* and *sola gratia* as Bultmann can state: 'The preaching of the faith does not bring a new concept of God, as if he were not the judge who demands good works, as if God were only benign. No! We can speak of God's grace (*járis*)

only when we also speak of his anger (*orgé*)': R. Bultmann, *Theologie des Neues Testaments*, 1948–53; Eng. trans. *Theology of the New Testament* (in one volume), New York: Prentice Hall, 1970; here Sp. trans, 1981, p. 218.

20. R. Otto, *Das Heilige* (1917); Eng. trans. *The Idea of the Holy*, Oxford: OUP, 1923.

21. Based on a public debate with a theologian friend, I wrote *Del Terror de Isaac al Abbá de Jesús* (Estella, 2000); a similar concern produced my *¿Qué queremos decir cuando decimos 'infierno?* (Santander, 1995).

22. S. Freud, 'Zeitgemäss über Krieg und Tod', in *Ges. Werke X*, 1915, p. 351; quoted by L. Maldonado, *La violencia de lo sagrado*, Salamanca, 1974, p. 80.

23. In J.-P. Changeux and P. Ricoeur, *Ce qui nous fait penser: la nature et la règle*, Paris: Odile Jacob, 1998; here Sp. trans., 1999, pp. 246–7.

24. P. Ricoeur, *La Critique et la conviction*, Paris: Esprit, 1995. Eng. trans. *Critique and Conviction*, New York: Columbia UP, 1998; here Sp. trans., 2003, p, 211.

25. Cf. F. Wilfred, 'Christianity and Religious Cosmopolitanism. Toward Reverse Universality', *Concilium* 2007/1, 112–22.

26. Letter dated 5 Mar. 1919; I have considered this in *La constitución moderna de la razón religiosa* (Estella, 1992), pp. 85–106.

27. W. F. Otto, *Theophania. Der Geist des altegriechischen Religion*, Hamburg, 1959; here Sp. trans., 1978, p. 20. He complains here of the narrowness of 'theologians' and 'scientists of religion'. Hume himself recognized that polytheism comes first *in fact*, but that monotheism does so *intellectually*, in that 'the order and framework of the universe, carefully examined, support this argument', even though human beings could not reach this level 'when they formed their first rude notions of religion' (*op. cit.*, I, p. 110). In Indian theology 'the basic image is of the one in the many' (see the articles by Cornille, above, and Amaladoss, below).

28. 'His [Moses'] aim is a political monotheism, a monotheism of alliance. [. . .] The existence of other gods is here completely accepted, unlike the case of Akhenaten. Otherwise, the requirement of faithfulness would make no sense. These other gods are not denied, but they are *forbidden*. Adoring them will not only be considered madness but the worst of sins' (Assmann, *op. cit.*, p. 46. The distinction from Akhenaten may be real, but *it cannot fairly be blamed on mono- theism*).

29. See M. J. Borg and J. D. Crossan, *The First Paul* (London and New York, 2009) concerning Christian monotheism's 'peace through justice' and love, compared to the 'peace through victory' in war of what I personally would call the 'impe- rial henotheism' of the Roman Empire.

30. Nineveh represented '[m]ore or less what the Third Reich means to Jews today': V. Mora, *Jonás*, Estella, 1981, p. 21. Assmann, significantly, argues with Nehemiah (*op. cit.*, p. 9) but does not mention Jonah.

31. For profound observations in discussion with Assmann, see J. Ottmar,

'Überlegungen zum Wahrheitverständnis des Monotheismus', in J. Ottmar and M. Möhring-Hesse (eds), *Heil-Gerechtigkeit-Wahrheit*. LIT, 2006, pp. 136–66.

32. A. Torres Queiruga, *Repensar la revelación*, Madrid, 2008 (first published in Galician, 1985); cf. *idem*, 'Rethinking Pluralism: From Inculturation to "Inreligionation"', *Concilium* 2007/1, 102–11.

33. L. Massignon, quoted by R. Caspar, 'The Permanent Significance of Islam's Monotheism', *Concilium* 177 (1985/1), 67.

The Triune God versus Authoritarianism

ERICO HAMMES

The main question to be examined here is the divine dimension of human equality as a condition for divine discourse. This is not a matter of colonizing the achievements of post-theocratic society, or of abrogating the principle of divine governance where it is postulated in present-day cultures. It is, though, a matter of clarifying the traditions of service and communion present in Christianity, without making any special claims in relation to monotheist understandings, which are analyzed in another article in this issue.

For human beings, the Ultimate remains always human. It is only insofar as it is human that the Divine is divine for us. Or, in terms of top-down theology: any transcendent reality can only reach human beings through being immanent, through approach and proximity. Following the Christian tradition, this is the form taken by divine self-communication: as Jesus Christ, as human being, existence, history, culture, and condition. The most Transcendent, conditioned to the reduced world of a brief, conflictive immanence, makes transcendence itself stutter in a new way. The grammar of Christian discourse about the Divine is tied to the stated involvement of the Word with the world of life and the life of the world, in such a way that the intimate relationship between their destinies is brought to light. Speaking of God is always speaking in human terms, and thinking of God is thinking of human beings.

Even while it is gratuitous and imprescindible, the divine approach means a surrender and an approach. The surrender, *livraison*, comes about in revelation, which always supposes someone in a history, in a culture, and in a communicative subjectivity of difference and similarity. The otherness that draws close, in communication, will always also be similar to the recipient. This is the descent of the divine in the form of the Word, or the word that forms the divine arrival. In a certain sense, the divine will always be conditioned by the disposition of the word to be able to be the distance that both places identity at a remove and reduces difference. The strange is integrated into the familiar, with the permanent risk of a God being turned into an idol.

Transported beyond themselves by their word, in the attempt to express their own limits in total otherness, human beings can discover their weakness in what remains, meanwhile, their possibility of being. Words become strange when they affirm the divine, and the only way of limiting their inherent ambiguity is to contemplate the face of the divine in its effects on ourselves.

I. Is there opposition between affirming the divine three-in-one and authoritarianism?

The term authoritarianism refers to a form of government concentrated on those who hold power.[1] Three contexts in which the term applies have traditionally been distinguished: power structures, psychological dispositions, and political ideologies. While *auctoritas* represents making others grow, authoritarianism is a means of exercising power by which other subjects in the group or community are reduced. It can be found among individuals, in families, in schools, in society, and in the Church. It is distinguished from absolutism, which is hardly a form of government but need not necessarily act against the population. Although its relevance may be debatable, there is also a distinction to be made from totalitarianism, in which power is concentrated in a single person or group. Authoritarianism is a form of relationship in which the interlocutors are reduced and the principle of authority is disfigured.

From the psychological point of view, a correlation between subservience and authoritarianism can be established.[2] Authoritarian personalities count on the submission of their underlings and behave in a servile manner toward those in authority over them. In the religious sphere, this form of relationship can be recognized in fundamentalism, fideism, and integralism. Sacred texts and traditions become mystified authorities, things one cannot make one's own, opaque to thought and reason.

Authoritarian ideologies, for their part, are characterized by denying validity to any differing expression of thought and by upholding the absolute validity of their own position. They generally march with contempt for and disqualification of any other way of seeing or thinking. Non-identical groups and classes, as well as races and cultures, are disregarded or eliminated. In recent history we can instance the abuses committed in the name of the French Revolution, of liberalism, collectivism, and especially Nazism, fascism, and their variants, the multiple military regimes on several continents, the messianic pretensions of some U.S. governments, and so many other forms of justifying ethnocentrism and manipulative monopolization and harsh repression of those 'who are not on our side' in the famous words of an American President.

When we examine the relationship between authoritarianism and trinitarian faith, we should remember that authoritarianism, like other forms of inter-subjective relationships, possesses its own dynamic and constitutes itself as a way of being-before-others capable of proposing a legitimizing theology – even one that makes appeal to the divine three-in-one. By eliminating any contradiction, authoritarianism also destroys any critique and its limits, even if these are the Divine Mystery. Still more easily, it resorts to the mechanism of hypostasization, the identification, that is, of exercise of power with transcendence itself. 'Being in' power is confused with 'being' the power and the negation of any contrasting power, including a divine other who is not the one with whom it identifies.[3]

It can be said that the only effective way of overcoming authoritarianism is to try out different forms of relationship. Such are experiments in participation, non-authoritarian, that can lead to a different exercise of power. They suppose the empowerment of all those involved in taking decisions and implementing them. 'Participative planning' and 'participative budgeting' have become current expressions in this form of taking power and overcoming subservience. At a global level, the World Social Forum has become a catalyst for implementing different models of power, capable of bringing new subjects and new faces to the global agenda. Resistance movements across the planet develop their own identity and make themselves visible in countermanding unilateral decisions characterized by a sort of *diktat* with authoritarian traces. This observation is obviously not designed to suggest a sort of Manichaeism, identifying, for example, the Economic Forum with authoritarianism and the Social Forum simply with its replacement. What one certainly can say, however, is that the two show a different way of relating to power.

It is before these new forms of power and in courageous acceptance of a polycentric and plural society that the *logos* on the Christian God needs to be re-evaluated, without claiming any new, and certainly authoritarian, justification. We shall need to seek a hermeneutic of power in the circle between the divine and the human. Perhaps we should seek not so much a theological critique of authoritarianism as a theology of critique of authoritarianism. In other words, when a group tries to resist authoritarianism, can it be supported with a corresponding theology? What would this theology be like? Would one model of trinitarian theology prove more resistant to authoritarianism than another? Or would we have to re-think the entirety of faith in the triune God in order to give an account of overcoming authoritarianism? The way here seems to require a two-handed approach: giving authority faith and giving faith authority. It has to be said, however, that a theology of non-authoritarian power requires a confrontation with our understanding of the divine mystery.

II. A mystery of transformation

As the recovery of trinitarian thought is very recent, its explicit presence in various resistance movements to authoritarian regimes hardly appears significant. During the Second World War, Dietrich Bonhoeffer stood out for his witness based on following Jesus, even though the Confessing Church and the Ecumenical Movement based themselves on Trinitarian faith.[4] In the 1960s the new political theology (Moltmann and Metz) defended critical freedom vis-à-vis the State on the basis of the eschatological reserve of the Reign of God, with its main emphasis on christology. Latin American liberation theology was inspired by the liberator God of the Old Testament and came to speak of Jesus Christ the Liberator (Boff, Sobrino), but Trinitarian reflection came on the scene later. In a similar fashion, the Social Teaching of the Church, in its understanding of the political community and its – ever diplomatic – critique of authoritarian forms of government, generally looks to natural law or human rights, to the right to authority founded on God, but not to an understanding of the Trinity. Such references to the divine mystery as exist – as in *Gaudium et Spes*, for example – tend to mention the Economic Trinity and not the Immanent. In other words, divine action is normative in the face of authoritarianism, but its essence is still not specified.

In the overall picture of Christianity the Pentecostal movement should not be forgotten, especially in its original forms, as a trinitarian movement working against authoritarianism. Insofar as it recuperates the pneumatological dimension, it gives Christianity back its freedom and charismatic capacity in the face of the structures of internal organization, but also the disposition to resist external imperatives. Something similar happens with the Catholic Church as a whole, to the extent that it understands itself as a community brought together and animated by the Holy Spirit, whether in the official documents of Vatican II or in regional synods and conferences. In its actual workings, lay movements from Catholic Action to the base communities display a consciousness of their own responsibility capable of enlivening and changing power relationships, both in society and the Church.

(a) The return of the divine three-in-one in pain and suffering

The Christian originality of trinitarian faith remained for almost a millennium on the margins of Christian consciousness. It is still very common to find church documents that speak of God in the abstract, inasmuch as explicit references to the three divine Persons are rare.[5] On the other hand, however, several Western traditions gradually rediscovered this train of thinking about the divine in its specifically Christian form: suffice to think of Karl Rahner and Karl Barth in the early second half of the twentieth century. In the following decades a vast quantity of works were produced across continents and contexts, to the point where it is now virtually impossible to make an exhaustive list of all the research projects and publications in this field. Without going into details, it is now valid to state that the Christian relationship with power changes if God is understood in a different way. Or, to be more precise: when we accept a different form of power, it will also be easier to re-think the divine mystery. So Congar could write in 1981: 'Today [. . .] if the Blessed Trinity is the source and model of anthropology and even of human or ecclesial society, it is so by taking it in the fullness of a consubstantial life of the three "Persons", and particularly by developing a Pneumatology which has too often been forgotten in what H. Mühlen has called a pre-trinitarian monotheism.'[6]

At the beginning of the third millennium of Christianity, amidst crises and searches, we can, then, observe the consolidation of a new period of trinitarian faith, shown within the Catholic Church also in the encyclicals of John Paul II and in some of his symbolic actions calling for a world of peace and solidarity. More recently, Benedict XVI, by taking up the charity-principle of the God-love, has established an essential criterion for considering reality and relationships from other angles.

On this return journey, we should not forget the part played by atheism, especially in the nineteenth century and the early years of the twentieth, with its radical critique of the threatening, alienating, and oppressive God.[7] From Marx to Sartre and Camus, via Freud and Nietzsche, who all brought a mass of workers and intellectuals with them, the God of the monotheists was harshly censured. In fact, the caricature that had survived from centuries of identification with absolutist regimes, with economic systems, means of production, civil and ecclesiastical power structures, and indeed life itself, made any peaceful co-existence virtually impossible. Hence Sartre's alternatives of God or freedom, the existence of God or the existence of human beings. The response would require a new theodicy first and foremost, in order to establish the possibility of upholding, not to say conceiving, the divine in its relationship with humanity. Paul Tillich and Edward Schillebeeckx, as well as political theology, liberation theology, and black theology, at different times and in different contexts, can all be read as part of a new dialogue between culture and thought and faith.

The first concern of the God of Christians and monotheism is his weakness. The faith and thinking that survived the concentration camps and the horrors of war developed the *logotherapy* (Viktor Frankl) of the pain of believing and being weak. Perhaps, to paraphrase Heidegger inappropriately, only a weak God can save.[8] This is why people are returning to the theme of suffering, not to isolate God but to discover him in his inner being. Standing next to God, when God is suffering, is, according to Bonhoeffer, the distinctive characteristic of Christianity. Kitamori's suffering God allowed Moltmann and then Sobrino to speak of transcendence in a different way. The cross comes to be the *locus* of re-encounter with Christian authenticity and also the negation of negation. The executioners will be left without God, and the victims will be God's tent.

(b) Beyond oneness: the communio of persons

In theological tradition, the Christian faith has to move between oneness and the baptismal symbol invoking the Father, Son, and Holy Spirit. For a long time, the West expressed oneness in terms of essence and the Trinity in the formula of persons. In this way, the concern and conviction of monotheism became predominant in its thinking, with the risk of a rigid defence of oneness. The concept of person, in its turn, was marked by Boethius' definition ('individual substance with rational nature'), leaving out the biblical echoes of countenance, visage, likeness. Over many centuries – perhaps excepting Eastern thought and, in the West, the spirituality, mysticism, witness to charity and dialogue of such figures as Nicholas of Cusa, Bartolomé de Las Casas, and many others – the general consciousness of Christianity was rather monotheist, with derivations justifying authoritarianisms and persecutions, than properly trinitarian. On many occasions, Christian faith in the one and triune God was understood as opposition to the belief of other peoples and cultures, or even, until quite recently, a hindrance to dialogue and encounter with other religions. As for the concept of person, an excessively individualistic understanding of it, focused on oneself, led to its being questioned by none other than Barth and Rahner, who were rightly concerned with rescuing theological reflection on the mystery of God.[9]

Of the three classical models for understanding the divine three-in-one – one nature in three persons (Western model); the Father as *the* God and origin of all divinity (Eastern model); communion model – I am going to consider mainly the last two here, on account of their intrinsic critique of authoritarianism.

In the biblical tradition, especially in the New Testament, reference to the Father, Son, and Holy Spirit enjoined the concept of a reality greater than a singular unity, the traditional concept of perfection, to express the divine. It was Tertullian who identified the possibility of conceiving the reality of the three in terms of persons, and so of a greater reality.[10] He was inspired in this endeavour by prosopographic exegesis (the dialogues among biblical characters) and also by experience of grammatical persons. On the one hand, *person* is seen as the 'not-other', as the identity of oneself and one's world; on the other, as openness and relatedness. Following Gisbert Greshake's synthesis, we can identity *hipóstase* and *persona* as the initial embodiments of the term 'person'. Even though the Bible spoke of *prósopon*, it was the term *hipóstase* that prevailed, on account of its metaphysical value.

After Tertullian, the Cappadocian Fathers established the same validity in God of unity and plurality, identity and difference, with the same origin. The *perichoresis* of the persons came to express the dynamic unity that stems from the Father as its origin. With Augustine, the concepts of relationship and love came to characterize the future of trinitarian thought, even if his stress on unity in essence led to a reception dominated by a reality pre-dating three-in-oneness. In general terms, in the light of history, we can recognize one form of trinitarian understanding as 'the personal differentiations in God are on the same level as and have the importance as God's unity, so that the differentiations are identical to God's essence as God',[12] with the persons at the same time being separate and related greatnesses. Autonomy, relatedness, selfhood and otherness, as well as inter-relationship of identity and difference, singularity and plurality – all go to the making of a 'person'.[13] In a certain sense, being a person in this manner requires an act of reception as something on its own. We might recall Richard of St Victor's *ex-sistere*, and *hipóstase* as such contains a principle of *en-hipostasia*: that is, of reception of others and of *insufficiency* in contrast to *self-sufficiency*, which is characteristic of authoritarianism.

How, then, does oneness manifest itself? And what is the nature of three-in-oneness?

The concept of *person*, summarized above, is correlative with the biblical and patristic concept of *communio, koinonia*. Even if two currents can be identified, one that starts from the meaning of the *perichoresis* of the persons, displaying a shared oneness, and another that takes up the Eastern tradition of the Father generating the Son and breathing out the Spirit, they coincide in essentials.[14] Etymologically, the term *communio* can be elucidated as similarity of conditions (*moenia*, wall, delimitation) and gift (*munus*), task, charge. The inter-personal relatedness consists in being in the life of another person, in sharing and receiving.

In the words of Jon Zizoulas, 'the person is otherness in *communio* and *communio* in otherness'.[15] It implies and requires the elimination of division in the face of difference: 'If we change difference into division, we die'.[16] Faithful to his Eastern Christianity, Zizoulas affirms the Father as the cause of *communio*, while at the same time nevertheless defending *communio* as being primordial in the Trinity.[17] The causality in question here does not relate to *ousia*, substance, but to otherness. The Father is cause because he causes the Son and the Spirit. Causality in this sense is concerned not with *what* but with *how* the Father is: the cause of otherness, through which the persons are distinguished in the divine mystery. Clearly, from the point of view of trinitarian theology and of a different understanding of the meaning of *communio*, we might ask to what degree the pericoretic reciprocity of the persons is upheld in this structure. Furthermore, does placing the ultimate source in the Father not lead easily to a subordination or even a sort of modalism in the reception of theology?

For Greshake, on the other hand, 'God is that *communio* in which the three divine persons, in the three-way interchange of love, bring about the one divine life as reciprocal self-communication.'[18] The ultimate reality of three-in-oneness is not, therefore, the Father, but the *communio* as mediation between oneness and multiplicity that is brought into being in the dialogue of love among the persons. Being love, as Eberhard Jüngel says, God is 'the actuality and history of making himself present', so '*this history of love* is God himself'.[19] Because this is how God is, Greshake concludes, there is no need to envisage a logical or ontological priority in the Divine Mystery.

The fact of God being three-in-one entails, in traditional terms, that, on the one hand, this constitutes a unity such that a greater cannot be conceived and, on the other, that the difference among the persons is such that a greater cannot be imagined.

III. Can we uphold three-in-one without authoritarianism?

The anti-authoritarian principle represents a radical critique of any oppressive theism and requires a new hermeneutics of the divine. In the case of Christian belief, the main achievement is the assertion of three-in-oneness as *communio* of persons and of 'communiality' as the personalizing principle. Communiality expresses the essential availability and bestowal of the divine to human beings, to history, to culture, to nature, and to what is different; it means the acceptance that constitutes the freedom to be and stay there.

The divine three-in-one, evidenced in the compassionate and serving existence of Jesus, carried to the extreme of falling victim to the authoritarian religious and political system of his time, demonstrates the radical weakness of one who became nothing in order to give place to something. Far from legitimizing the forces of domination, he showed them the opposite – obedience unto death, even on the cross. Becoming the last is being the least and the place from which it is possible to speak of the greatest mystery. In this way, the principle of peace and fullness is brought in.

The characterization of persons as 'being-for-others-and-with-others' stands over against the annihilating 'being-above' of authoritarianism and countermands the will to enslave others. To say Father, Son, and Holy Spirit means allowing someone to be other than oneself, and to make oneself an other for someone, to give a name and surname, to baptize, to make oneself a sister and brother, to draw close to the poor, to widows and orphans, to strangers and to what appears alien, so that even our enemy has a place and a life.

Whether one is thinking of society, Church, school, or international and cultural relationships, or those between men and women, or between generations and races, the communial-agapic divine unity sheds light on hope for a living together in difference and with real authority, *auctoritas*, which makes people live and grow. The God of others will then no longer be a God forbidden to others, and far less can others be destroyed for the sake of one's own God, because believing in the three-in-one that is love means allowing God to be greater than the understanding we have of him, while in the God of others we recognize the God we do not possess.

The three-in-one conceived of in this way does not represent a God we have to explain, or that has to be deduced from physics or metaphysics; neither quantum physics nor the theory of relativity can impose his existence; nor does he even need to be the principle of 'intelligent design', sufficient reason for the origin and evolution of life. This God allows himself to be seen by those who have eyes and a heart, understanding and reason, capacity for encounter, and veneration for existence.

Translated by Paul Burns

Notes

1. Cf. 'Authoritarianism', in *Encyclopedia Britannica* and other major reference works. There is also wide coverage of its application in the field of education. For its links with religion, see M. Zafirovsky, *The Protestant Ethic and the Spirit of Authoritarianism: Puritanism, Authority and Society*, New York: Springer, 2007.
2. Besides the observations of Hannah Arendt on the banality of evil, intrinsically linking it to subservience, and Theodor Adorno's study of the authoritarian personality (1950), see R. Altmeier, *The Authoritarians*, Winnipeg: University of Manitoba, 2006 (available online), and the thesis by G. Norris, *The Authoritarian Personality in the Twenty-First Century*, Robina, Queensland: Bond University, 2005 (available online).
3. 'For them [authoritarian doctrines] the ordering of society desired is not a hierarchical structuring of functions created by human reason but an organization of natural hierarchies sanctioned by the will of God': 'Authoritarianism', in N. Borobio, *Dicionário de política*, vol. 1, Brasília: UnB, 200, p. 96. According to the same article, de Maistre (1753–1821) saw 'divine providence' underlying human affairs, for which reason, 'people should be educated in the dogmas of faith and not in the illusory exercise of reason'. God, and not the sovereignty of the people, is the source of power. For other authors with similar views, such as Donoso Cortés (1809–53), 'sin is the nostalgia for chaos' and the fount of such evils as liberalism, democracy, and socialism.
4. One should perhaps recall that, on the other hand, the 'German Christians' (*Deutsche Christen*), allied with Nazism, proposed a Christianity without Judaism, and therefore without an understanding of the God of the Old Testament. This tendency can also be found in other attempts to buttress authoritarianism and, above all, to justify persecutions, religious or otherwise.
5. Cf., *e.g.*, the 'Aparecida Document' from the Fifth General Conference of the Latin-American and Caribbean Episcopate (13–31 May 2007).
6. Y. Congar, 'Classical Political Monotheism and the Trinity', *Concilium* 143, *God as Father* (1981), p. 35, referring to H. Mühlen.
7. Both J. Moltmann, in *The Crucified God*, and E. Jüngel, in *God as the Mystery of the World*, refer to the debate with atheism.
8. According to Heidegger, 'Only a God can save us' (*Nur noch ein Gott kann uns rekken*): interview in *Der Speigel, Sonderausgabe, 1947–97*, pp, 284–5, published posthumously. 'All that remains for us to do is prepare our readiness in thinking

and poetizing (*im Denken und Dichten*) for the appearance of God or his absence in disappearance', he continued.

9. On the continuation of the debate in H. Vorgrimler and others, se H. Hoping, 'Deus Trinitas. Zur Hermeneutik trinitarischer Gottesrede', in M. Striet (ed.), *Monotheismus Israels und christlicher Trinitätsglaube*, Freiburg: Herder, 2004, p, 128–52; *idem*, 'Die Selbstvermittlung der volkommen Freiheit Gottes', in P. Walter (ed.), *Das Geweltpotential des Monotheismus und der dreieine Gott*, Freiburg: Herder, 2005, p. 166–77.

10. On this point see B. J. Hilberath, *Der Personenbegriff der Trinitätstheologie in Rückfrage von Karl Rahner zu Tertulians 'Adversus Praxean'*, Vienna and Innsbruck: Tyrolia, 1986.

11. Cf. G. Greshake, *Der dreieine Gott: eine trinitarische Theologie*, Freiburg: Herder, ⁵2007, pp. 172–82.

12. *Ibid.*, p. 172.

13. Personalist and 'I-thou' philosophies (as in M. Buber, G. Marcel, E. Mounier, E. Levinas, among others) have by various routes largely coincided with the understanding of 'person' sketched here.

14. For what follows, cf. esp. J. Zizousias, *Being as Communion*, Crestwood, MO: St Vladimir's Seminary Press, 1997; *idem*, *Communion and Otherness*, London and New York: T. & T. Clark, 2006; G. Geshake, *Der dreiene Gott, op. cit.*. Among other works by like-minded theologians, we should mention Moltmann, esp. *The Trinity and the Kingdom of God;* L. Boff, *Trinity and Society;* E. Cambón, *Assim no terra como na Trindade*; E. A. Johnson, *She Who Is: The Mystery of God in Feminist Theological Discourse*.

15. Zizousias, *Communion and Otherness*, p. 9.

16. *Ibid.*, p. 9.

17. Cf. *ibid.*, p. 126.

18. Geshake, *Der dreiene Gott*, p. 179. For what follows, see pp. 182–216.

19. Cf. E. Jüngel, *Gott als Geheimnis der Welt*, Tübingen: J. C. B. Mohr, 1986, p. 449.

The One Spirit and Many Gods

MICHAEL AMALADOSS

The Spirit is a source of pluralism in the Christian tradition. The recognition of the presence and action of the Spirit in other religions may lead us to see the many Gods of different religious traditions as manifestations in history and culture of the One Absolute beyond name and form. This is the substance of the argument that I shall try to lay out in the following pages.

In the Bible the Spirit appears as the divine creative force. Hovering over the primal void she presides over the emergence of the cosmos. She inspires the prophets and kings to become mediators of divine power in the course of history. She overshadows Mary when the Word becomes human in her womb, descends on Jesus at his baptism, and initiates his public ministry. Jesus acknowledges the power of the Spirit in him as he proceeds to proclaim and realize the good news among the poor. He promises the gift of the Spirit to his disciples to help carry on the work of the Reign of God. The Spirit is indeed the wisdom and the power of God that animates the realization of God's plan in the world. She is the power within the cosmos and the humans, inspiring and creating.

I. Speaking in many voices

The Spirit appears as a source of pluralism on the day of Pentecost. Mary and the disciples of Jesus – about 120 of them – were gathered in the upper room. The Spirit comes upon them in the form of a strong wind and tongues of fire resting on each of them. 'All of them were filled with the Holy Spirit and began to speak in other languages, as the Spirit gave them ability' (Acts 2.4). The gathering crowd is bewildered. There were people from all parts of the Mediterranean wondering, ' How is it that we hear, each of us, in our own native language?' (Acts 2.7).

Here we see two kinds of pluralism. First of all, the disciples speak in tongues. The same message is communicated in different languages to different groups of people. It is often suggested that this is the contrary of what happened at the tower of Babel. When people were getting together to assert their power independent of God, the diversity of languages broke up their unity and provoked their dispersion. Now people speaking different languages are coming together as one community responding to the same message. The diversity of languages is not suppressed. People do not miraculously understand the message proclaimed in one language, say Aramaic. Rather, people hear the same message, each in her or his own language. The diversity of languages is affirmed. But it does not become a factor for division. The Spirit is conveying the same message through the different languages. The message is exposing God's deeds of power, which starts a new age in which young men shall see visions and old men shall dream dreams. The gift of the Spirit is promised to all who are ready to repent. The repentance is shown in their breaking of bread together and celebrating community (cf. Acts 2). Here we see the many becoming one without losing their differences rooted in their languages. This is the miracle of the tongues.

There is also a second kind of pluralism here that is rarely noted. There were 120 disciples in that upper room when the Spirit came upon them. The power of the Spirit must have been manifested in these 120 people in different ways. There were the mother and brothers of Jesus and other women and men followers. The narrative in the Acts focuses on Peter and the other apostles. It quietly ignores the various prophetic charisms of the many others, especially the women, present in that group.

II. Many charisms in one community

Paul, in his letter to the Corinthians, attends to this variety of charisms forced by the tensions in that community. He writes: 'Now there are varieties of gifts, but the same Spirit; and there are varieties of services, but the same Lord; and there are varieties of activities, but it is the same God who activates all of them in everyone. To each is given the manifestation of the Spirit for the common good' (1 Cor. 12.4–7).

He then goes on to list some of the charisms and concludes: 'All these are activated by one and the same Spirit, who allots to each one individually just as the Spirit chooses' (1 Cor. 12.11). Then follows an affirmation of equality and community. 'In the one Spirit we were all baptized into one body – Jews or Greeks, slaves or free – and we were all made to drink of one Spirit' (1 Cor. 12.13).

Paul's point here is that every charism is the gift of the Spirit for the service of the community. They are different but equal. So they should not be the cause of conflict, considering some as superior to the others. In our context here I would emphasize this focus on the fact of the plurality of charisms, equal in difference and oriented to the service of one community. Paul's use of the image of the body in this context could become problematic, if it is interpreted in a hierarchical sense opposing the body to the head.

III. Beyond institutional borders

The Spirit is also the inspirer and agent of another kind of pluralism. The apostles saw their experience of the life, death, and resurrection of Jesus in the context of the Jewish tradition. They did not immediately perceive its relevance for the others. It is the Spirit that leads them to understand that the good news of Jesus is for all humans, not only the Jews. The Acts narrates for us the story of how the Spirit delicately leads Peter to the house of Cornelius (Acts 10). The invitation comes from Cornelius. Peter is prepared by the vision which warns him not to call unclean anything created by God. As Peter is telling the story of Jesus in the house of Cornelius, the Spirit takes the initiative of giving herself to the 'pagan' household. Peter and his companions 'were astonished that the gift of the Holy Spirit had been poured out even on the Gentiles, for they heard them speaking in tongues and extolling God' (Acts 10.45–6). Peter has no choice but to celebrate the gift of the Spirit symbolically by baptizing them. He explains the event to the others back in Jerusalem: 'If then God gave them the same gift that he gave us when we believed in the Lord Jesus Christ, who was I that I could hinder God?' (Acts 11:17). Here we see the Spirit manifesting another kind of pluralism: the eschatological gift of the Spirit is not merely for the Jews, but for all peoples in the world.

IV. The Spirit of freedom

The pluralism of the Spirit is rooted in her freedom. She is not bound by our structures and dividing walls. We need to be reborn in the Spirit to become members of the reign of God. But the Spirit is free to blow where she wills. Jesus affirmed this to Nicodemus: 'The spirit blows where it chooses, and you hear the sound of it, but you do not know where it comes from or where it goes. So it is with everyone who is born of the Spirit' (John 3.8). We tend to limit the Spirit to a particular community, culture or religion. We may even claim power over her. But she is free. Paul affirms this freedom of the Spirit in his letter to the Romans: 'All who are led by the Spirit of God are children of God. For you did not receive a spirit of slavery to fall back into fear, but you have received a spirit of adoption. When we cry "Abba! Father!" it is that very Spirit bearing witness with our spirit that we are children of God, and if children, then heirs, heirs of God and joint heirs with Christ' (Rom. 8.14–17).

This freedom is not something given but to be acquired and experienced. It is a process. Creation itself participates in this process and becomes free (cf. Rom. 8.22). The Spirit also helps us in our weakness and prays in us. 'And God who searches the heart, knows what is the mind of the Spirit, because the Spirit intercedes for the saints according to the will of God' (Rom. 8.25). Freedom in the Spirit is opposed, on the one hand, to the obligations and institutional structures of the Law and, on the other, to the 'flesh', as the principle of human weakness (cf. Rom. 7). 'You are not in the flesh; you are in the Spirit, since the Spirit of God dwells in you' (Rom. 8.9).

The Spirit therefore is the principle of freedom and creativity, pluralism and community. She is the presence and action of God in us humans and in the cosmos. She 'blows where she chooses'. It is in this experiential faith context that we have to explore the implications of the presence of the Spirit in other religions and cultures.

V. The Spirit in other religions

The Second Vatican Council makes a very broad statement about the presence and action of the Spirit in human beings. In its document on 'The Church in the Modern World' (GS), after describing the action of the Spirit in the Christians, it affirms: 'All this holds true not only for Christians but also for all people of good will in whose hearts grace is active invisibly. For since Christ died for everyone, and since all are in fact called to one and the same destiny, which is divine, we must hold that the Holy Spirit offers to all the possibility of being made partners, in a way known to God, in the paschal mystery (22e).

While affirming the centrality of the paschal mystery in the event of salvation, the Church suggests that a participation in this mystery is possible for all, in ways unknown to us, but known to God, through the Holy Spirit. Theologians such as Karl Rahner would suggest that the various religions may actually be the locations where such a divine-human encounter takes place, given the social-symbolic nature of human beings.[1] This is confirmed by John Paul II in his encyclical *The Mission of the Redeemer*:

The Spirit manifests himself in a special way in the Church and in her members. Nevertheless, his presence and activity are universal, limited neither by space nor time (DV 53). . . . The Spirit's presence and activity affect not only individuals but also society and history, peoples, cultures and religions. . . . Thus the Spirit, who 'blows where he wills' (cf. John 3.8), who 'was already at work in the world before Christ was glorified' (AG 4), and who 'has filled the world, . . . holds all things together (and) knows what is said' (Wis. 1.7), leads us to broaden our vision in order to ponder his activity in every time and place (DV 53). . . . The Church's relationship with other religions is dictated by a twofold respect: 'Respect for man in his quest for answers to the deepest questions of his life, and respect for the action of the Spirit in man.' (28–29)[2]

VI. The other religions and the Church

How do we understand the presence and action of the Spirit in human hearts and other cultures and religions? We can see two approaches that seem to be in tension. One approach tends to link the work of the Spirit not only to the paschal mystery of Christ, but also to the Church. John Paul II says:

> Whatever the Spirit brings about in human hearts and in the history of peoples, in cultures and religions serves as a preparation for the Gospel and can only be understood in reference to Christ, the Word who took flesh by the power of the Spirit, so that as perfectly human he would save all human beings and sum up all things. The universal activity of the Spirit is not to be separated from the particular activity within the Body of Christ, which is the Church. Indeed, it is always the Spirit who is at work. Both when he gives life to the Church and impels her to proclaim Christ, and when he implants and develops his gifts in all individuals and peoples, guiding the Church to discover these gifts, to foster them and receive them through dialogue. (29)

There is of course no problem with such an interaction between the Church and various other religions. But the question is whether the other religions need to have a historical link with the Church (and Jesus). It seems that they need not. For John Paul II also says:

> Since salvation is offered to all, it must be made concretely available to all. But it is clear that today, as in the past, many people do not have an

opportunity to come to know or accept the Gospel revelation or to enter the Church. The social and cultural conditions in which they live do not permit this, and frequently they have been brought up in other religious traditions. For such people salvation in Christ is accessible by virtue of a grace which, while having a mysterious relationship to the Church, *does not make them formally part of the Church* but enlightens them in a way which is accommodated to their spiritual and material situation. (10)

Here a mysterious relationship with the Church is affirmed – which obviously is not historical. So we have a pluralism of religions animated by the Spirit. The document *Dialogue and Proclamation* is more clear and forthright. It says: 'Concretely it will be in the sincere practice of what is good in their own religious traditions and by following the dictates of their conscience that the members of other religions respond positively to God's invitation and receive salvation in Jesus Christ, even while they do not recognize or acknowledge him as their Saviour.'[3]

The Spirit of God, therefore, is present and active in other religions. This activity is related, in ways unknown to us, but known only to God, to the paschal mystery. But it is not related to Jesus as known and experienced in faith by us, or to the Church as a visible, historical institution. This means that various religions facilitate salvific divine-human encounter in various ways. We can see this as a manifestation of the pluralism characteristic of the Spirit of God. The Spirit is at the source of the pluralism of religions. This is made possible by the freedom of the Spirit 'who blows where she wills' and the freedom of those who respond to her in various cultural and historical ways. The unity of humanity in the salvific plan of God at the level of mystery is manifested and realized in multiple ways at the level of history, cultures, and religions. Since it is difficult to speak of this pluralism with reference to the historical Jesus, it is attributed to the Spirit. But let us remember that where the Spirit is the Father and the Word are also.

Religions and the Spirit of God

It is in this context that we can attempt to gain a little more clarity about how actually the Spirit of God is operative in the various religions and cultures. The document *Dialogue and Proclamation* speaks of the 'sincere practice of what is good in their own religious traditions'. What does this mean? The reflections of Indian theologians over two related issues are worth recalling here. They have had two seminars: one on 'The Inspiration of Non-biblical

Scriptures'[4] and the other on 'Sharing Worship'.[5] The first concluded that the other religious scriptures can be considered inspired and so used in Christian liturgy. If the Spirit of God is present in other religions, she must have spoken through their scriptures, though the message was primarily addressed to their followers. The second said that we can participate in the worship of other religions since all religions worship, through various symbols, the one God. An act of faith in what is happening will obviously be required. Both these conclusions depend on the acceptance of other religions as facilitating salvific divine–human encounter through their proper scriptures, symbols, rituals and institutions. The Spirit of God, active in them, enables such divine–human encounter.

From such a perspective we can say that the Gods of other religions are various manifestations of the one God. They are not mere idols, but real mediations. They are not merely different 'names' of one and the same Reality. They are actualizations in a people's history and culture. They represent interventions of God in their history. The people narrate such interventions and re-live them in sacred times and places and through appropriate images. These give the Absolute a name and a form. Their worship is directed not to these images, but through them to the Absolute that they represent and mediate. So when we are looking at the many religions in the world and their Gods, we are not really encountering many Gods, but many historical, cultural, and religious manifestations of the one God.

VII. One God in many manifestations

Once this principle of pluralism in unity at the level of God and her manifestations is accepted then we can envisage the possibility that there can be many manifestations of God within the same religious tradition. Among the many religions known to us, Hinduism makes provision for such a possibility. The *advaitic* (non-dual) tradition speaks of the Absolute-without-qualities (*Nirguna Brahman*) and of the Absolute-with-qualities (*Saguna Brahman*). The *Saguna Brahman* is the manifestation of the *Nirguna Brahman* and can be many. At the level of manifestations a pluralism is possible for personal, historical, and geographical reasons. The *advaitic* theologian Sankara has beautiful devotional songs to Siva, Vishnu, and Devi (the Goddess). Saiva Siddhanta is another non-dual school. In its tradition, Siva has many manifestations in different places under different circumstances to different people. The many manifestations are expressed in various images installed in various places. They have their local histories and commemorations. But they are many forms or manifestations of one Siva. In the tradition of *Vishnu*, the Absolute takes many *avatars* or manifestations to restore righteousness in the cosmos on different historical occasions. It is traditional to speak of ten *avatars*, with the tenth one still to come. These avatars are worshipped as divine manifestations. But there is no doubt in the devotee's mind that they are manifestations of one God – *Vishnu*. In an atmosphere of such a variety of Gods and Goddesses in India, at a popular level one tends to relate them to each others as members of one large divine family. But the wise sages would insist that they are manifestations of the one Absolute. The actual way that the relationship between the many and the one is understood depends on various philosophical worldviews and presuppositions. The basic image is that of one-in-the-many. From such a perspective the Hindus find it easy to integrate the Gods of other religions into their system.

There is a surprising Christian parallel, even if it is only hypothetical, to this vision. Asking whether many incarnations are possible, St Thomas Aquinas answers: 'The power of a divine person is infinite, not limitable in regard to anything created. So, [. . .] we must hold that beside the human nature actually assumed, a divine person could take up another numerically distinct' (ST 3,3,7). We believe today only in one incarnation of the Word of God in Jesus. Since the whole cosmos participates in the paschal mystery there is no need for other incarnations. But in principle other incarnations are possible. If, on the model of Jesus, each incarnation is seen as a divine-human person then we will have many human incarnations of one divine person. We would not certainly consider them as many Gods, but as different incarnations of one God. The unity of God will not be affected by God's many incarnations.

Conclusion

We see in the Bible the Spirit of God as the principle of freedom and pluralism not limited by human, historical structures. Though the New Testament speaks only of the pluralism of tongues and charisms, the Church today evokes the presence and action of the Spirit to understand the pluralism of religions. But to accept religious pluralism is to acknowledge the diversity of divine manifestations in the religions, considered Gods by them. Since God is one, these can only be different manifestations of the one Absolute.

Notes

1. Cf. K. Rahner, *Theological Investigations*, Vol. V, London: Darton, Longman & Todd, 1969, p. 128.
2. The references in the text are to *Dei Verbum* (DV) and *Ad Gentes* (AG) of the Second Vatican Council.
3. No. 29.
4. See D. S. Amalorpavadass (ed.), *Research Seminar on Inspiration in Non-Biblical Scriptures*, Bangalore: NBCLC, 1974; M. Amaladoss, 'The Scriptures of Other Religions: Are They Inspired?', in *Beyond Dialogue*, Bangalore: ATC, 2008, pp. 69–78; G. Gispert-Sauch, 'Vatican II and the Use of Indian Scriptures', in J. Kavunkal (ed.), *Theological Explorations*, Delhi: ISPCK, 2008), pp. 35–48.
5. See See P. Puthanangady (ed.), *Sharing Worship. Communicatio in Sacris*, Bangalore: NBCLC, 1988.

A New Vision – Liberating without Excluding, Specific without Identity

ERIK BORGMAN

Both the Bible and the Koran are unequivocal in stating that we should worship only one God. As a key figure and exemplary believer in Judaism, Christianity, and Islam, Abram/Abraham/Ibrahim leaves his country, his kindred and his father's house, answering to God's word and travelling to the land that God promises to show him (Gen. 12.1). Thus he witnesses to an unconditional and exclusive faith in the self-revelation of the transcendent God. Our contemporary situation, sometimes called post-modern, seems to show in a sense the return of the gods once left behind by Abraham, or even – as the Ibrahim story in the Koran narrates – smashed. The sociologist Max Weber already suggested that in the modern rationalized world that is in his view in a sense the cultural product of monotheism, the gods of polytheism would return to haunt us.[1] Of course, one could respond to this with cultural criticism and the demand to stay with the tradition. But this may be too superficial a response. What should we think of the Egyptologist Jan Assmann, who analyzed monotheism as a strategy that bans God from everywhere else in order to give the authorities of monotheistic religion the monopoly of representing God's presence? Christian theology, according to Assmann, is inextricably related to this logic of monotheistic religion. It intends to expose false gods who are supposedly everywhere, presenting the God of one's owns tradition as the true and only one. Assmann calls this the violence inherent in monotheism, of which it has to be stripped to regain its credibility. In Assmann's estimation, this is impossible without giving up monotheism itself.[2]

Assmann's criticism is topical, because claiming to proclaim a liberating God, the Christian tradition cannot be credible if it depends on subjecting people to silence, presenting their experiences and expressions of the religious as *a priori* irrelevant or theologically and morally wrong. Claiming to voice the protest of those who are excluded and suffer, against their exclusion and their suffering, theology should not be founded on exclusion and the suffering that comes with that. At the same time, however, this very argument itself depends on a criterion that is considered to be universal: the true God cannot endorse repression. And, to drive home my point, this seems exactly what is implied in the 'Hear Israel, YHWH is our God, YHWH is one; and you shall love YHWH our God with all your heart, and with all your soul and with all your might'. It is the confession that only the liberating God that was revealed in the Exodus from Egypt is worthy of worship. This liberating God will in the end prove to be the God of heaven and earth.

I. The plural ways of missing the one true God

This is exactly how Johann Baptist Metz stresses the importance of God's unity and uniqueness. For Metz, God is either a theme for humanity as a whole, or not a theme at all: 'Gott ist entweder ein Menschheitsthema, oder überhaupt kein Thema'. Speaking of God should be universalistic not on the basis of an abstract philosophical idea of a true God as necessarily unique, but because of the universality of suffering that can only be redeemed by universal liberation.[3] The point is that *all* tears have to be wiped away, as is promised twice in the book of Revelation (7.17; 21.4). In my view, this opens possibilities for a non-exclusive idea of God's uniqueness. And that is what we need in order to remain true to the biblical tradition.

It has been shown in some detail that the biblical confession to God as the 'one-and-only' differs fundamentally from what is commonly understood as 'monotheism': the theoretical insight that there is and logically can be only one God. The idea of a 'biblical monotheism' is therefore to a large degree a modern misunderstanding.[4] But what does this mean for systematic theology? Metz's disciple Tiemo Rainer Peters has called the political theology of his mentor a 'Theologie des vermissten Gottes', a theology of God missed.[5] I think that is a very fortunate expression, and not just for indicating Metz' project. In the biblical tradition God is proclaimed present in people missing God, searching for God, crying for God and God's redeeming presence. The history of which we are part clearly indicates that God still has not fulfilled our human yearning and is therefore not indisputably present, not even in Jesus Christ and his history. This is exactly what incarnation and *kenosis* mean: God accepted the conditions in which God's salvation is never unequivocally realized. According to Metz' political theology, remembering Jesus' suffering, death, and resurrection in this situation means keeping open the unbridgeable chasm between our actual history and the liberating holiness of God's Name, to which all the earth will sing a new song when it is universally revealed. Speaking of the Crucified as the *kenotic* incarnation of God's presence means confessing to every revelation of that chasm as also revealing the paradoxical presence of God's universal will to save.[5] In other, even more paradoxical words: God is *one* and *universal* and *unique* because God is present in all the *different* traces of yearning and hope for redemption, in all their *multiplicity* and *pluralism*. God's unity cannot be conceptualized but is present and hidden in the plurality of experiences of missing the fullness of liberation God's presence stands for, according to the Christian tradition.

Theologically speaking, with the vulnerability of our bodies and the violence present in our world, we are already dedicated to and dependent on the God of redemption. But in order for this dedication to make sense and for this dependence not to be a sign of the unavoidable victory of death and nothingness, the power of God should be universal, all-encompassing. God should be the one-and-only, and nothing should be excluded from God's nearness and God's power. This may be what is suggested when the biblical tradition confesses to the God of redemption as the one and only, passing final judgment among the gods – at least this is how I read Psalm 82. Amidst and connected with the abundant plurality of principalities and powers, God is hidden as the one speaking the final, righteous judgment that means universal redemption and revelation (cf. Col. 2.5).

II. The plural revelation of God as the one-and-only

In other words, the revelation of God as the one-and-only is historical because incarnation and *kenosis* mean that God is connected with history. The pain of missing God reveals God's presence and nearness. The Jewish philosopher Peter Ochs has connected this idea to the Christian image of God as Trinity.[6] In his view, talk of the Trinity is the way in which the Christian tradition bears witness to the fact that it is a living religion. Talk about the God revealed in Jesus the Anointed One always arises from the presence of the Holy Spirit, which time and again makes people experience new, unexpected, and unprecedented traces of the God Jesus revealed. In Ochs' view, Jewish thought about the relationship among God, Law (Torah), and the People of the Covenant has a similar structure to the Christian thought of the relationship in God's presence as Father, Son, and Spirit. Religion offers space to live in confrontation with the uncertainty, fragility, and uncontrollability of existence. In Christian terms this emerges from the nearness of the Spirit of the God who created heaven and earth as space for good life, who has emptied himself in Jesus' human and deathly history, and was incarnated in a body that suffered and died from the fact that the world as it really exists is often in no conceivable sense such a space. The Spirit opens up new life in our seemingly closed and clearly deadly world ever again, in ever new and unexpected ways.

The Catholic-Hindu philosopher and theologian Raimundo Panikkar has pointed out the opacity and impenetrability of the presence of the Spirit if it is understood in this way.[7] The connection of what are considered to be traces of God here and now to the history of Jesus' life, death, and resurrection is often unclear and remains hidden. According to Panikkar, however, this should not lead to the rejection of these experiences in the name of an alleged identity of the Christian Church, or of the God it confesses and is called to represent. We should not be more strongly attached to the Christian identity than Jesus was to his. As the Apostle writes: 'Have this mind in you, which was also in Christ Jesus, who, existing in the form of God, counted not the being on an equality with God a thing to be grasped, but emptied himself' (Phil. 2.5–7). This means that we should hold on firmly to the idea that – in my words – because of this emptying the God of Jesus is the God of heaven and earth, of history and of each individual personally. As long as the end of history has not dawned, the pluralism of views, experiences, and longings cannot be reduced without cutting off essential insights into God's being, gained in the humble human life which God in Jesus made his dwelling-place.

This is by no means to say that we should give up the idea of God's unity and have to be content with the given plurality of revelations of the divine. It does mean that we do not know what the exact character of God's unity is and that we are still searching for it, on our way toward it. The Christian confession that God was in Jesus in a unique manner, and that in him God's face has come to light in ways that cannot be equalled or surpassed, does not imply that we know what that means and implies. The significance of God's revelation in Jesus' history only becomes clear in the ongoing process of confrontation of what we think we know with old and new experiences we ourselves and others have had, even if they seem at odds with them. Or, to put it in trinitarian language, the unity of the Father, the Son, and the Spirit that is the identity of God can be known in our human history only in the interaction between our experiences of and reflections on the three divine hypostases, and the relations between them.[8] Any insight we express about these things is at the most a snapshot in the midst of an ever-ongoing movement. Which means that we know what it means to be connected to that movement, which as a movement reveals unity but not what the movement as a whole entails and thus not what its unity is.[9]

III. The plural presence of the one and only end

At the end of the Gospel of Matthew (28.19), Jesus says to his apostles: 'Go and make disciples of all the nations, baptizing them into the name of the Father and of the Son and of the Holy Spirit'. This is not a mission to subject people to a closed ideology and prescriptive identity, as if the whole world is supposed to become what confessing Christians already are.[10] It is a mission to invite others to invest their lives in the search for what it means that the God of Jesus is the God of heaven and earth, and is therefore in the process of unifying our history in the liberating reality of that what the Gospels of Mark and Luke call the Kingdom of God, the Gospel of Matthew calls the Kingdom of Heaven, the Gospel of John calls Eternal Life, and the Apocalypse calls a New Heaven and a New Earth, and a New Jerusalem coming down out of heaven from God, in irreducible diversity and unmistakable unanimity.

Notes

1. M. Weber, 'Die protestantische Ethik und der Geist des Kapitalismus' (1904–5), in *idem, Gesammelte Aufsätze zur Religionssoziologie* I, Tübingen: J. C. B. Mohr, [9]1989, pp. 17–206, here 203–6.

2. See esp. J. Assmann, *Herrschaft und Heil : Politische Theologie in Altägypten, Israel und Europa*, Munich: Hanser, 2000; *idem, Die Mosaische Unterscheidung: Oder der Preis des Monotheismus*, Munich: Hanser, 2003.

3. See J. B. Metz, 'Theologie versus Polymythie oder: Kleine Apologie des biblischen Monotheismus', in *Einheit und Vielheit*, ed. Odo Marquard, Peter Probst, and Franz Josef Wetz, Hamburg: Meiner, 1990, pp. 170–86. Cf. also *idem*, 'Im Eingedenken fremden Leids: Zu einer Basiskategorie christlicher Gottesrede', in *idem*, J. Reikerstorfer, and J. Werblick, *Gottesrede*, Münster: Lit, 1996, pp. 3–20; *idem*, 'Im Pluralismus der Religions- und Kulturwelten: Anmerkungen zu einem theologisch-politische Weltprogramm', in *idem, Zum Begriff der neuen Politischen Theologie: 1967 – 1997*, Mainz: Matthias-Grünewald, 1997, pp. 197–206.

4. For an overview of research in Old Testament studies on monotheism, cf. F. Stolz, *Einführung in den biblischen Monotheismus*, Darmstadt: Wissenschaftliche Buchgesellschaft, 1996; R. K. Gnuse, *No Other Gods: Emergent Monotheism in Israel*, Sheffield: Sheffield Academic Press, 1997; M. Th. Wacker, '"Mono-

theismus" als kategorie der alttestamentische Wissenschaft: Erkenntnisse und Interessen', in J. Manemann (ed.), *Monotheismus*, Münster: Lit, 2002, pp. 50–67.

5. T. R. Peters, *Johann Baptist Metz: Theologie des vermissten Gottes*, Mainz: Mattias-Grünewald, 1998.

6. Cf., for Metz's christology, P. Budi Kleden, *Christologie in Fragmenten: Die Rede von Jesus Christus im Spannungsfeld von Hoffnungs- und Leidensgeschichte bei Johann Baptist Metz*, Münster: Lit, 2001.

7. P.W. Ochs, 'Trinity and Judaism', *Concilium* 2003/4, pp. 51–9; cf. also *idem*, 'A Jewish Reading of Trinity, Time and the Church: A Response to the Theology of Robert W. Jenson', *Modern Theology* 19 (2003), 419–28.

8. R. Panikkar, 'The Jordan, the Tiber, and the Ganges: Three Kairological Moments of Christic Self-Consciousness', in J. Hick and P. Knitter (eds), *The Myth of Christian Uniqueness: Toward a Pluralistic Theology of Religions*, Maryknoll: Orbis Books, 1987, pp. 89–116.

9. Thomas Aquinas underlines that whereas to human persons their relations are accidental, to the divine persons in the Trinity the relations are part of the essence. In other words, God is one in the trinitarian relations between Father, Son and Spirit (ST I, Q. 39, art. 1). The idea that speaking of God in terms of Father, Son, and Spirit means that we cannot yet comprehend the specific unity of God in our history, is the basis of the reflections on the Trinity in F.-W. Marquardt, *Was dürfen wir hoffen, wenn wir hoffen dürften? Eine Eschatologie*, III, Gütersloh: Kaiser/Gütersloher Verlaghaus, 1996, pp. 212–35; *idem, Eia, wärn wir da! Eine Utopie*, Gütersloh: Kaiser/Gütersloher Verlaghaus, 1997, pp. 539–66.

10. Cf. also my article 'Opening up New History: *Jesus of Nazareth* as the Beginning of a New History', *Concilium* 2008/3, pp. 64–72.

Part Three: Theological Forum

Karl Rahner's Work Twenty-five Years Later: A Lasting Legacy and Challenge

PAUL EPPE

On 30 March 1984 Karl Rahner died, a Jesuit among Jesuits, in Innsbruck, his elective place of residence. Cardinal Lehmann, one of his pupils, considers him to have been one of the 'epoch-making theologians of the twentieth century'.[1] In a tribute for Rahner's seventieth birthday, his friend and student Johannes Baptist Metz referred to the 'mystical biography of a Christian'.[2] In 1974, when he was still Cardinal Ratzinger, Pope Benedict XVI called Rahner's major work *Foundations of Christian Faith: An Introduction to the Idea of Christianity* (*Grundkurs des Glaubens*) a 'great book' that will 'outlast transient fashions in theology and remain a noteworthy . . . source of inspiration when much contemporary theology is long forgotten'.[3]

In his lifetime Rahner produced an immense number of written and spoken works – about five thousand in all. It is not too fanciful to compare his theology to a series of volcanic eruptions. They emanated in the mystical depths of a divinely-enlightened awareness and reached the surface by processes both transcendental and metaphysical, to emerge as forms of expression singularly appropriate not only to a Christian but to an extra-Christian environment. This transformation always arose from personal involvement. Karl Rahner was never primarily an observer and thought of himself accordingly as a pastoral theologian with a mission, and not as a neutral scholarly theologian. His constant concern with divinely-directed human existence, with humanity as the essential subject of theology, was a major contribution to the movement toward an anthropologically centred theology. For him all theology started with human beings, which means that theology exists only for human beings.

Do the life and work of Karl Rahner arouse less interest twenty-five years after his death? Not at all. We have to give a resoundingly positive answer to those who ask if this great practitioner of an emphatically transcendental and mystical theology and advocate of the Second Vatican Council (1962–5) still has anything to say to us today. As *peritus* to Cardinal König of Vienna, Rahner was undoubtedly a major influence on the conception and shaping of the forward-looking results of the Council that were to supply the Church with a new internal and external dynamic thrust. He was also one of those who, with pioneering enthusiasm and great personal commitment, worked in the very front line of that movement to ensure the consistent practical implementation of conciliar outcomes. Therefore his permanent legacy is directly evident in the results of the Council, which we might summarize essentially as amounting to nothing less than a transformation of our understanding of Church and world. Consequently, the Church in assembly is primarily aware of its task and commission as a universal Church. It opens itself to the real world but also begins to recall the fact that God cannot be more precisely defined either in biblical and dogmatic or in epistemological and metaphysical terms (*deus semper maior*), and therefore to realize that what Rahner repeatedly referred to as 'absolute and inconceivable mystery' is central to all searching for God. Now the formerly predominantly doctrinaire magisterial Church talks in relatively mild tones, and in Rahner's sense, of salvation as universally applicable to all people of good will and any faith. When the Council was over, Rahner also spoke in decidedly euphoric terms of the 'beginning of a beginning', and therefore of the onset of a new beginning, although he also remarked that, 'It will take a long time before the Church that received the gift of the Second Vatican Council becomes a Church of the Second Vatican Council'.[4] These were prophetic words, for even now the Church is only at the beginning of the process of implementing the Council, and under the present pontificate we cannot even be sure that it will seriously initiate any such procedure. That is not all. It was mainly after the Vatican instruction *Donum vitae* (Gift of Life, 1987), that people began to opine that the official Church had already started to back a return to the past (e.g. in liturgical reform). And now, to cap it all – certainly contrary to the spirit of Vatican II – Benedict XVI has confirmed the episcopal status of a Holocaust-denier. Even the subsequent denials of the Vatican errors and confusion that caused distress across the world give pause for thought. What is left of Rahner's euphoria about a new post-conciliar approach to theology, a new form of salvific thinking open to the world and intended to embrace all humankind? The following is a short account of some key points that are essential for any understanding of Rahner's conception of theology in association with conciliar thinking.

In his analysis of human being (spirit in the world), Rahner focuses on the philosophical notion that human beings are a question in themselves, for they have a 'need' to inquire about God. In *Spirit in the World* (*Geist in Welt*), his first work on the metaphysics of being, human beings are said to realize themselves primarily as believers. Ultimately, by 'spirit in the world', Rahner always means 'God in the world'. The fundamental assumption to be derived from this proposition accompanied all Rahner's later work: everyone can perceive God, even when he is silent, as Rahner points out in *Hearer of the Word* (*Hörer des Wortes*). God's revelatory self-communication to human beings lies essentially in this perception of him – even if he is silent. That is the 'specific, the sole, centre of Christianity and its message'.[5] It was only much later, in *Foundations of Faith* (*Grundkurs des Glaubens*), that the the-ocentric approach with its emphasis on the direct awareness of God was combined with a special theology of grace and transcendental christology, with Jesus Christ as 'mediator of salvation', that Rahner devised on a basis of faithful rational thought. His theology, especially with reference to the Incarnation, is 'anthropology *sub specie aeternatis*'. It aims at an anthropologi-cal localization of biblical revelation, but ultimately divides – according to Cardinal Ratzinger's profound insight of 1978 – into a first and second stage theology.[6] We can also say that Rahner talks of God's self-communication to the human creature as an individual basic or initial revelation, so that the biblical-dogmatic revelation, as it were, endows the primary revelation with eschatological significance. Accordingly, Rahner was also able to attribute the following words to Ignatius, the founder of his Order, in a supposed message to a 'present-day Jesuit': 'Are you not surprised to learn that . . . my mysti-cism has allowed me such certainty of faith that it would remain unshakable even if there were no Holy Scripture?'.[7] It is scarcely surprising that this kind of paradigmatic 'shift' in theological perspectives also evoked funda-mental criticism on the part of the Roman magisterium. Rahner's change in theological method did not sort with the fundamental cast of the magis-terium and the Church's self-conception. Rahner's thinking was certainly aligned with that of the Council, but even at that point it also ranged far beyond Vatican II. I shall say no more about this, but confine my remarks to Rahner's continuing relevance for us today.

In this regard we should return to the historical starting-point. With his particular theological and philosophical approach, Karl Rahner stands at the beginning of an era that admittedly cannot demonstrate God's existence, but is just as incapable of denying it. The path in question led by way of Kant, Nietzsche, and Heidegger on the one hand, and by way of Schleiermacher, Kierkegaard, and the 'New Theology' on the other hand, to reach the anthropological turning-point in theologizing. We might say that Kant had to abrogate knowledge in order to make room for faith; that after the death of God Nietzsche asked somewhat helplessly who was to fill the empty space; and Heidegger was unable to 'nullify' the ultimate nothing. Rahner's theology of faith is always primarily theological anthropology. From the start it is established essentially and aboriginally, that is, constitutively, in human nature as a 'supernatural existential', and is personally experienced as faith, so that it directly affects and 'concerns' the human being experiencing it. That is, from the very start God is always cited simultaneously – consciously or unconsciously – in human thinking, and this notion of God within and with us is considered and interpreted in human language. This is the only way to understand Rahner's theologumena, that of the 'supernatural existential' of humankind and that of 'anonymous Christianity', both of which stress the immediate God-directedness of human beings. In this respect, Rahner is describing something akin to a global City of God (*civitas dei*), in which the Christian scriptural message is a transcription or interpretation of God's self-revelation (self-communication) to human beings experienced in a transcendental and mystical mode.

The ecumenical relevance of this theological anthropology is unmistakable. Not only did Rahner commit himself indefatigably to the unity of Christian Churches on the basis of this fundamental idea, and usually as the sole commentator on these particular lines, but he also showed a sympathetic interest in the 'God' of other religions. In *Foundations of Christian Faith* he goes so far as to talk of 'Jesus Christ in non-Christian religions' and of the 'searching memory of all faith' (that is, *memoria*, or 'an *a priori* principle of expectation, of searching, of hoping'),[8] which is always directed to the absolute saviour. From this fundamental theological viewpoint, the transcendent God is always the 'absolute and incomprehensible mystery' that can certainly be experienced, even though humans cannot understand it, even analogously.

In fact, there is support for maintaining that this notion of human knowledge is possible only by means of a transcendental-mystical theological thinking that can dispense not only with a claim to unique universal validity in matters of faith but with narrow dogmatic pronouncements on them. Pope Benedict XVI in his Regensburg address (2006) recommended an extension of the concept of reason, and Rahner's transcendental-theological notion of God could offer the very approach demanded by the papal exhortation. The pronouncements of Vatican II on freedom of conscience and religious freedom (*Gaudium et Spes* 16ff and *Dignitatis Humanae*) also call for further reflection in this direction. Thus official church theology is encouraged to proceed much more courageously along the lines of faithful rational thinking. The Church as a social institution *sui generis* is not located above but in the world. According to Rahner its task can only be to promote and accompany the advance of humans toward salvation. The conciliar pronouncements on the universal nature of salvation (*Gaudium et Spes* 22; *Nostra Aetate*) offer appropriate guidance in this respect. This idea is not only a conciliar recommendation but a course encouraged by a certain current in philosophy. Two examples will help to make this clear.

Gianni Vattimo has referred to a 'new receptivity to the religious' and a 'rebirth of religion'[9] and, in answer to the question 'Is there such a thing as a world without God?', follows Heidegger's *Being and Time* (*Sein und Zeit*) in locating the gateway for secularized post-modern thinking about God beyond Christianity in 'weak thinking'.[10] In conclusion, he poses the doubtless rhetorical question 'whether here we cannot find significant suasions for more positively and effectively combining the philosophical concern to overcome metaphysical objectivism with the search for an understanding of Christianity that finally would also be capable, not only on a dogmatic but on an ethical level, of conceiving of one's own ecumenical awareness primarily as paying full attention to the new – post-modern – era of being'. Quite apart from the religiously amenable Gianni Vattimo, we should heed Jürgen Habermas, who, though not religiously inclined, nevertheless remarks (for instance in *Zwischen Naturalismus und Religion*,[11] his collection of essays on aspects of the philosophy of society and State) that in essence the principle of tolerance is an indispensable and fundamentally supportive and sustaining principle in the religious sphere too. Tolerance in this sense means that naturalism and religion, knowledge and faith, must study, critically investigate, and define each other reciprocally in the socio-political environment. This gives rise to the need for a secularizing form of adaptation favouring an effectively democratic form of State – an outcome also prompted by the realization that faith and knowledge, reason and religion have to engage in mutual scrutiny if they are to avoid any overweening self-satisfaction. Therefore a major trend in contemporary philosophical reflection encourages consideration of the basic socio-political and cultural value of religion and faith. Surely this tendency accords fundamentally with Rahner's secular impulse and that of Vatican II, that is, their desire to open up to the world, holding as they do that since the beginning of creation God (as God in the world) has never ceased to accompany humanity on its way to salvation.

As a pastoral theologian, Rahner constantly reminded and still reminds us that theology is never an end in itself and should never be pursued in isolation. It must always serve a faith that human beings understand, freely accept, and can use to direct their lives. In that sense, he still advocates a theology that is capable of 'forgetting faith' to a considerable degree. He reminds us of the need for the Church to be open to the world and to look openly at the world, in awareness of its salvific task of accompanying humanity by 'helping people to help themselves'. Consequently, even twenty-five years after his death, Karl Rahner would advise the leaders of the Roman Catholic Church to locate their duty of service more emphatically in the present-day world. His message is still that it is God himself who has always addressed human beings, and continues to do so, in faith or in the anonymity of life as it is actually lived.

Translated by J. G. Cumming

Notes

1. K. Lehmann, 'Karl Rahner', in H. Vorgrimler & R.v.d. Gucht (eds), *Bilanz der Theologie im 20. Jahrhundert, Bahnbrechende Theologen*, Freiburg: Herder, 1970, pp. 143–76.

2. J. B. Metz, 'Exkurs: Theologie als Biographie', in *Glaube in Geschichte und Gesellschaft*, Mainz, 1977, pp. 195–203.

3. J. Ratzinger, 'Vom Verstehen des Glaubens, Anmerkungen zu Rahners Grundkurs des Glaubens', *ThRv* 74 (1978), 177–86.

4. K. Rahner, *Das Konzil – Ein neuer Beginn* (address given in Munich in 1965), Freiburg, 1966.

5. *Idem*, 'Erfahrungen eines katholischen Theologen', in K. Lehmann (ed.), *Vor dem Geheimnis Gottes den Menschen verstehen*, Freiburg, 1984, pp. 105–19, 109ff.

6. J. Ratzinger, *Der christliche Glaube und die Weltreligionen* (*Gott in Welt, Festgabe für Karl Rahner*, vol. II), Freiburg, 1964, pp. 287–305.

7. K. Rahner, 'Rede des Ignatius von Loyola an einen Jesuiten von heute', in *Schriften zur Theologie*, Vol. XV, Zurich, Einsiedeln & Cologne, 1969, pp. 373–408.

8. K. Rahner, *Grundkurs des Glaubens, Einführung in den Begriff des Christentums*, Freiburg, 1984), pp. 303–12; *Foundations of Christian Faith*, tr. W. V. Dych, London & New York, 1978, pp. 311–21.

9. G. Vattimo, *Glauben – Philosophieren*, Stuttgart, 1997, esp. pp. 7–18.

10. *Idem, Jenseits des Christentums, Gibt es eine Welt ohne Gott?*, Ulm, 2004.

11. J. Habermas, *Zwischen Naturalismus und Religion, Philosophische Aufsätze*, Frankfurt, 2005, esp. pp. 258ff.

Monotheism and the Language of Violence: The Theological Debate over Jan Assmann's *Moses the Egyptian*

ROSINO GIBELLINI

Debate over the identity of God has a long history in Western philosophy.[1] In its latest phase, opened toward the end of the twentieth century, it has taken the shape of critique of biblical, Christian, and Islamic monotheism and of a renewed plea for a form of polytheism. This was started with the publication of the Egyptologist Jan Assmann's book *Moses the Egyptian. The Memory of Egypt in Western Monotheism* (Harvard University Press, 1997), followed by a German translation, *Moses der Ägypter. Entzifferung eines Gedächtnisspur* (Hanser Verlag, 1998) and then translations into other major international languages, mainly based on the (revised and enlarged) German edition.[2]

Assmann does not put forward a historical reconstruction of the figure of Moses,[3] but a 'mnemohistory', in the form of an examination of the figure of Moses in Western memory of him, derived mainly from the biblical Exodus, as the inventor of monotheism. The Moses of Exodus brings about a revolutionary development: from polytheism to monotheism. But in doing so, the biblical Moses takes up the Egyptian revolution of Amenophis IV, who called himself Akhenaten and in the fourteenth century BC founded a monotheistic religion, which was abolished after his death. This was an expression of a crisis of polytheism in antiquity. This interpretation builds on some intuitions expressed by Sigmund Freud in his *Moses and Monotheism* (1934–8), which holds that Moses was not a Hebrew but an Egyptian nobleman, a zealous follower of the monotheistic faith Amenophis IV imposed as the state religion around 1350 BC, later re-worked and focused on the symbolic figure of the Moses of Exodus. The Egyptian Moses thereby becomes the Moses of Exodus, and it is the Moses of Exodus who introduces monotheism into Western culture. The Pharaoh Amenophis IV brought about a revolution in the history of religion: he instituted the rigorously monotheistic cult of the

Sun God, whom he called Aten, thereby changing the entire cultural system of Egypt, which was polytheistic. But the revolution of Amenophis IV, Akhenaten, collapsed after his death, and Egypt 'happily' reverted to polytheism, in the form of a 'cosmotheism', which divinized the various forces of nature. The biblical Moses opposed this 'cosmotheistic' expression of Egyptian polytheism by introducing a rigorous monotheism, characterized by what Assmann calls 'the Mosaic distinction' between truth and falsehood, between true and false religion, a distinction unknown to polytheism. This distinction goes back to Akhenaten, but he could not impose it. It fell to the biblical Moses to bring monotheism to the West, which means precisely that the distinction between true and false, which might have been called the 'Akhenaten distinction', is now, rightly, called the 'Mosaic distinction'.[4]

Assmann's analysis depends entirely on his contradistinction between polytheism as cosmotheism and monotheism. Mosaic monotheistic religion is brought in under the banner of the commandment, 'You shall have no other gods' (Exod. 20.3; Deut. 5.7) and functions as a counter-religion in confrontations with polytheism. Polytheism is plural; it divinizes the plurality of the forces of nature; it is a natural religion; it is cosmotheism, in that it divinizes everything. The gods of polytheism/cosmotheism could be transposed from one culture to another: 'The sun god of one religion is easily equated to the sun god of another religion, and so forth. Because of their functional equivalence, deities of different religions can be equated'.[5] The gods of polytheism are international, by virtue of this translatability. 'Well known cases are the *interpretatio Latina* of Greek divinities and the *interpretatio Graeca* of Egyptian ones. [. . .] The powerful influence of this insight [translating divine names] can be seen in the field of international law . . . Intercultural theology became a concern of international law'.[6]

Monotheism, introduced by the Moses of Exodus, acts as a counter-religion by introducing the 'Mosaic distinction', meaning the criterion of truth or falsehood, unknown in polytheistic religions, which enabled it to stigmatize polytheism as paganism, idolatry, false religion, thereby ushering in the principle of religious violence. Polytheism was inclusivist; monotheism is exclusivist. Polytheism was worldly and optimistic; monotheism is intolerant and violent. Furthermore, the Mosaic distinction also brought in the concept of sin, opposed to the 'moral optimism that eats its bread with joy':[7] 'From the Egyptian point of view, sin seems to have come into the world with the Mosaic distinction, and this is perhaps the most important reason for calling it into question.'[8]

One of the first and most frequent objections to Assmann's book has been an appeal to historical reconstruction, while Assmann attends not to events but to 'mnemohistory', which is a history not of events but of memory of events. Assmann himself is well aware of this, as shown by his quoting, in a later work in which he re-visits his text, Peter Schäfer's objection: 'In reading these things, the reader must feel rather like the leper in the story of the rich man and the leper. Every time someone brings an argument against his historical reconstruction, Assmann cries, "But that's where I'm at! I'm well aware of it, but I'm not speaking of history; I'm dealing with the memory of history"'.[9] Schäfer here seems to be suggesting that Assmann's work is well founded but still lacks insights from other disciplines, such as history of religion and biblical exegesis.

In the field of biblical exegesis, it is worth referring to the closer analysis made by the Old Testament scholar Erich Zenger.[10] He accepts that Assmann's book represents a 'radical challenge' and a 'salutary provocation' to biblical discourse on monotheism,[11] which should be paying more attention to the post-modern mindset, highly attuned to pluralism. But he makes two criticisms: 'Assmann *overestimates* the peacefulness of polytheism': the wars of the great empires have been waged with the special help of their gods.[12] Equally, 'Assmann *overestimates* the "operative capability" of monotheism'.[13] The violence documented in history, attributable above all to Christian and Islamic monotheism, cannot be minimized, but what Zenger challenges is that violence is 'of itself' inherent in biblical monotheism. It is a matter of understanding the Mosaic distinction more deeply and in context: it is not primarily between the true God and false gods, but between freedom and slavery. The God of Exodus promotes resistance against slavery and leads to liberation. Here we can adduce the corroboration of liberation theology's reading of the Book of Exodus, which provides the biblical *topos* of its discourse.[14]

For Jürgen Moltmann, whom Pannenberg sees as having introduced a 'new trinitarian thinking' into theology,[15] the term 'monotheism' should not be introduced into this debate, on account of its ambiguity, the term 'theism' being ambiguous. There can be mono-, eno-, poly-, panen- theism, but the problem remains: What God are we talking about? The term dates from the Enlightenment: Hume uses it to describe the religion-of-dominion of the Persians, and therefore in the sense of a political monotheism, which as *Ur-Monotheism* has a long history – political, philosophical, and religious.

The monotheism of Exodus, however, is one of alliance and the *shekinah*, which has nothing in common with Pharaonic monotheism: 'If one confronts the divine indwelling among the Israelites with the creator of heaven and earth, one should speak either, with Abraham Heschel, of a bi-polar concept of God, or, with Franz Rosenzweig, of a self-differentiation. The one God, which Israel confesses, is then a God differentiated in himself.'[16] Christians may speak of a 'trinitarian monotheism', but if we go to the heart of Christianity we find the person and gospel of Christ. Then, the God of Jesus Christ is not the monarch, the God of the powerful, but 'the God of little ones', whom he brings into communion with God: 'The new experience of life acts in Christianity in the same liberating fashion as the experience of the exodus in Israel. If the latter provides the experience of liberation from the Egyptian theocracy, the former provides liberation from the power-without-God of death. Hegel was right to call Christianity "the religion of freedom".'[17]

Assmann's thesis has been closely examined by the Münster theologian Jürgen Werbick,[18] who claims that post-modernism has adopted polytheism as a metaphor for the multiple prospectivity of life (Nietzsche), as opposed to the professed absolutism of monotheism. For Assmann, the truth is incurably monotheistic, whereas our democratic cultures are pluralistic. We have to recognize that the truth of the God of monotheism can lead to a monotheistic truth-fanaticism, but in this case we would be dealing with a 'usurpative monotheism', in Nordhofen's expression.[19] But when we speak of God's truth in the biblical-theological sense, this refers to the truth about human beings (Ireneaus' *gloria Dei vivens homo*) and their destiny/destination, thereby activating resistance against the forces of evil and dehumanization. The whole course of twentieth-century Christian theology, in its basic themes, shows that it has placed itself at the defence and service of the '*Humanum*'.[20]

Assmann is aware of the critiques made of his thesis by theologians. He writes: 'My thesis has met with active and sustained resistance on the part of theologians, and yet Pope Benedict XVI, when still Cardinal Ratzinger, honoured it with a discussion, which was – truth to tell – quite fair and generous.'[21] Ratzinger went straight to the heart of Assmann's thesis, which is the 'Mosaic distinction', which, referring also to Greek philosophy, he suggests calling 'the Mosaic-Socratic distinction':[22] 'With this, one fact has been perceived in a certainly correct fashion: the question of what is true and what is good cannot be separated. If it cannot be distinguished from non-good, the good too becomes unrecognizable; the distinction between good and evil loses its foundation.'[23] Following on from here, he criticizes the solution proposed by Assmann of 'return to Egyptian pluralism' in the form of Spinoza's *Deus sive natura*, adding a theological lesson on 'freedom (the ideal pursued by modernity) being rooted in the truth of our being human'.[24]

These objections have made the author of *Moses the Egyptian* reflect, and his later publications have contextualized his thesis better: 'Today, more than two thousand years later, it is important to make clear that the violence of monotheism was not a necessary outcome of it [. . .]. It is not in the hands of believers that the stick of semantic dynamite contained in the sacred texts of the monotheistic religions explodes, but in those of fundamentalists who aspire to political power and who use religious arguments to drag the masses with them.'[25] And, furthermore, he suggests moving beyond distinctions (including the Mosaic distinction) to recapture the wisdom of 'deep religion': 'This is the wisdom with which men such as Mendelssohn and Lessing were imbued, or Schweitzer, Mahatma Gandhi, and Rabindranath Tagore in the twentieth century, and which we need to raise on high.'[26]

Translated by Paul Burns

Notes

1. Cf. J. Werbick, *Gott verbindlich. Eine theologische Gotteslehre*, Freiburg–Basel–Wien: Herder, 2007.
2. J. Assmann, *Moses the Egyptian. The Memory of Moses in Western Monotheism*, Cambridge, Mass. and London: Harvard U.P., 1997. (See author's comment on translations: not all his quotations are found in the English original, so some references are to the Italian edition, *Mosè l'egizio. Decifrazione di una traccia di memoria*, Milan: Adelphi, 2000, ²2007 – *trans.*).
3. Cf. E. Otto, *Mose. Geschichte und Legende*, Munich: Beck, 2006.
4. Assmann, *Moses the Egyptian*, see pp. 1–8.
5. Assmann,.*op. cit.*, see pp. 4–5; Ital. ed. p. 19.
6. Assmann, *op. cit.*, see pp. 45–6; Ital ed. pp. 74–5.
7. Assmann, *op. cit.*, Ital ed. p. 288.
8. *Ibid.*
9. J. Assmann, *Non avrai altro Dio. Il monoteismo e il linguaggio della violenza*, Bologna: Il Mulino, 2007, pp. 53, 141 n.
10. E. Zenger, 'Was ist der Preis des Monotheismus? Die heilsame Provokation von J. Assmann', *Herder Korrespondenz* 55 (2001) 186-191; refs to Ital. trans. in *Humanitas* 57 (4/2002) 576–84.
11. Zenger, *art. cit.*, 576, 584.
12. *Ibid.*, 580.
13. *Ibid.*, 581.
14. Cf. R. Gibellini, *The Liberation Theology Debate*, London: SCM Press, 1987.

15. Quoted in J. Moltmann, *Weiter Raum. Eine Lebensgeschichte*, Gütersloh: Gütersloher Verlagshaus, 2006.

16. J. Moltmann, 'Kein Monotheismus gleicht dem anderen. Destruktion eines untanglichen Begriffs', in *"Sein Name ist Gerechtigkeit"*. *Neue Beiträge zur christlichen Gotteslehre*, Gütersloh: Gütersloher Verlagshaus, 2008, pp. 83–96; here 89.

17. Moltmann, *art. cit.*, 90–91.

18. J. Werbick, 'Absolutistischer Eingottglaube? Befreinde Vielfalt des Politheismus?', in T. Söding (ed.), *Ist der Glaube Feind der Freiheit? Die neue Debatte um den Monotheismus* (QD 196), Freiburg–Basel–Wien: Herder, 2003, pp. 142–75. Cf. also K. Müller, 'Der Monotheismus im philosophischen Diskurs der Gegenwart', *ibid.*, pp. 176–213.

19. Cf. J. Werbick, *op. cit.*, p. 169.

20. Cf. R. Gibellini, *La teologia del XX secolo*, Brescia: Queriniana, 1992, enlarged [6]2007, pp. 559–60.

21. J. Assmann, *Non avrai altro Dio, op. cit.* (note 9), pp. 122–3.

22. J. Ratzinger, *Fede, Verità, Tolleranza. Il cristianesimo e le religioni del mondo*, Siena: Cantagalli, 2003, pp. 223–75; here 237.

23. Ratzinger, *op. cit.*, p.227.

24. Ratzinger, *op. cit.*, p. 269.

25. J. Assmann, *Non avrai altro Dio*, p. 128.

26. Assmann, *ibid.*, p. 131.

The Christian Humanism of Simone Weil: The Teramo Convention, December 2008[1]

MASSIMILANO MARIANELLI

Interest in the thought of Simone Weil (1909–43) is still strong a hundred years after her birth, and she continues to present a challenge and a summons to culture and to the Church. She can, without fear of exaggeration, be called one of the outstanding figures of the twentieth century. A pupil of the philosopher Alain (1868–1951), who taught numerous French intellectuals of the last century, Simone was a secondary school teacher and trade unionist. An enemy of all forms of totalitarianism and deeply critical of all idolatries, she opposed those she called 'day-dreamers', individuals prepared to do anything, to commit any crime, in order to achieve simply their own dream.

Simone worked in the Renault car factory, joined the 'Durruti brigade' in the Spanish civil war, and was then exiled to America, on account of her Jewish origins, even though, as she often declared, she was remote from Jewish culture and traditions. She then settled in London and became involved in the French resistance. She developed tuberculosis while still in England and died in Ashford Sanatorium in 1943. She is a figure who, as Attilio Danese and Giulia Paola di Nicola have stressed, 'escapes all classification, a stumbling-block to ideologies, contrary aggrandisements, and the failures of post-modern culture. Communist and anti-communist, agnostic and mystic, pacifist and warrior, intellectual and manual worker, Simone exercises a deep fascination on Western and Eastern cultures through her witness to her inter-cultural and inter-religious vocation: "I should betray truth were I to abandon the position I have found myself in since birth, which is the interstice between Christianity and everything that lies outside it."'

119

I. Man

Weil made 'man', seen always in an ontological-relational context, central to her thinking. In this context, presupposed by a renewed humanism and a renewed anthropological understanding, human beings find themselves in the situation of being able to make just one truly liberating and saving choice: that of 'tying at least [their] own love to the things of here below'. The tie that links freedom to salvation, freedom to human joy-realization, was a major constituent of Weil's anthropology, especially in the final phase of her short life. (The title of Maria-Clara Bingemer's book on her, *Simone Weil: quando a palavra è açao e paixao* – 'when word is action and passion' – is significant in this respect.) 'I am convinced that unhappiness on one hand and joy on the other, joy as total and pure adherence to perfect beauty, both entail the loss of personal existence and are therefore the only two keys that can open the gates of the pure land, the breathable land, the land of the real'; this 'pure' and 'real' land is what Weil calls the 'supernatural' dimension. She sees the possibility of freedom as passing always through renunciation of personal existence and the cause of the 'I': the 'I' should give way to the Other and be prepared to be like a 'nothing' of love for others. 'The dumb compassion of the Father for Christ. This compassion for each other is what a pure soul experiences in misfortune. A pure soul experiences the same compassion faced with others' misfortune. The love that unites Christ Abandoned on the cross to his Father across an infinite distance dwells in every holy soul. A part of such souls is solidly next to the Father.'[2]

In this context, clearly, Weil is criticizing any concept that places the individual as possessor of personal rights at its centre and denies the supernatural roots of sociability. She is convinced that only an outpouring of spirituality can be at the roots of any great civilization and of a renewed humanism. In this sense, Weil reveals her own opposition to personalism, demonstrating her preference for 'the impersonal'; there is nevertheless a constant dialectic between the two terms in her thinking. It is just this dialectic that allows the person to escape from personalism and the impersonal from cold neutrality.

II. Truth and myths

Despite the multiplicity of her interests, her work has a constant theme in her attempt to encompass the various aspects of reality such as expressions 'of the truth' like 'breath [. . .] sent by the Father'. So she writes: 'We should not speak of love of truth, but of a spirit of truth in love': truth is a gift that 'is always present in real and pure love'.[3] Such truth is 'the originator', the source of all saying and doing. 'God is the source of reality', she states, and so all spiritual, artistic, musical, and poetical productions and, in a special sense, myths, are led back to this originating truth. Myth is 'the narrative space of relationships' that lies at the root of all Weil's relational human-ism. Myths are accounts that, in exemplary form and better than any other literary genre, express joys and sorrows that the whole of humankind has experienced and continues to experience. These – handed down in various forms and languages – have to do with a certain human activity and together are the reflection of the supernatural, of the Word. 'The Word', Weil writes, 'is God's silence in the soul. It is the Christ in us.' Furthermore, qualifying the origin of all spiritual production, she writes: 'The cry of Christ and the silence of the Father together compose the supreme harmony, that of which all music is but an imitation'.

It is precisely in myths, considered as 'the narrative space of relationships', that, in my view, what we might describe as a 'Weilian universalistic human-ism' is founded. This humanism pays attention to 'culture' as a constitutive element of a people and of human development, thereby, we might say, in some way reclaiming the ideal of a properly humanistic 'culture'.[4]

'Culture', however, is, in Weil's view, not only the product of human intel-lectual activity, which constitutes the 'historical memory' of a people: in some manner culture itself also, and indeed above all, refers back to a spir-itual presence and to the dimension of the Sacred. This is a presence that can be qualified not only as a 'common sense' or 'universal sense' but more correctly as that 'unique essence' that Weil sees as lying at the origin of all cultures and traditions: this means, we might say, the spiritual root gathered into every past cultural and religious tradition.

III. Simone Weil and the Church

As already anticipated at the international convention on Simone Weil held in September 2007 in Rio de Janeiro and clarified at the recent Teramo con-vention, light has been shed on a particularly controversial aspect of Weil's existential-spiritual journey: her hesitation before Baptism. At Teramo, Eric O. Springsted, professor at Princeton University and a Presbyterian pastor, stated: 'Simone Weil was baptized, as directly witnessed by Simone Deitz, the friend who poured water on her forehead and recited the Church's formula with Simone's consent'. In at least two letters Simone Weil had set out the reasons for her refusal of Baptism. According to Springsted, 'It was a matter of fear of belonging to a group, including the Church, because, she maintained, the herd instinct has the capacity for ruling out moral thought and imagination'.

It was not till 1960 that rumours that she had been baptized *in extremis* by a lay person began to circulate. The fact that she was baptized does not remove, as Danese has opportunely observed, Weil's previous objections, especially her philosophical ones, 'in which she asserted that the Church's demand for intellectual adherence to dogma as a condition for receiving baptism was unjustified. There is no reason to think she had abandoned these objections.'

At the Teramo convention, the Jesuit Piersandro Vanzan addressed the subject of the difficult relations between Simone Weil and the Catholic Church, still unresolved among critics, and which Weil saw, rightly or wrongly, as the reason for her 'threshold' vocation. He pointed out that she chose to anchor herself heart and mind to the unitary essence of the great religions, leaving aside dogmas, institutions, ecclesial groupings, declarations. She felt the need to reach the divine through the 'negative way' that remains the secret of those souls that seek God. This is why Simone's life and works provide a disturbing provocation, not only in her radical and vigorous critique of modern culture, but also as a fruitful challenge to possible developments in the Church.

IV. Christ and the seeds of the Word

The role Weil allotted to myths and religions throughout the course of her intellectual and spiritual journey seems to leave room for ambiguity about the role of Christ, and she would appear to oscillate between the superiority of Christ over the other traditions and the presence of figures that possess the same value as him. The ambiguity can be overcome, in my view, by viewing Christ himself as the unity of past and present: as divine Word, Christ would embrace the whole history of humankind, and the various mythic figures would be no more than anticipations of him or, in other words, seeds of the Word. In Weil's religious universalism, particularly in her last works, Christ (it seems to me) is the only *metaxy* (intermediary) in the full sense of the word, and, as Wanda Tommasi among others has shown, for Weil it was only in clinging to the cross that 'the universe regains meaning and can reveal its symbolic structure'.[5] In effect, Weil states that Christ is the 'main gate' to cognition and the key to understanding the universe and human destiny: 'We can truly understand the universe and the destiny of men', she writes, 'in particular the effect of misfortune on innocent souls, only by perceiving that these have been created, the one as the Cross, the others as the brothers of the crucified Christ'.[7] Only once these have been transformed into so many mediators, thanks to their sharing in the *eikon* of Christ, can we read the symbols of the universe and those of other religious traditions as revelations of the divine. Weil writes: 'We must imitate Christ, because our calling is to be mediators. Mediators between God and the reality of which our feelings form the very structure. As the very being of God is to be goodness – God is not a being to whom goodness is tied as an attribute, but absolutely pure goodness – so the very being of the sensible world is to be sensible.'[8]

Christ is then the model of 'absolute emptying', and through him it is possible to establish communication between the 'sensible world' and the Absolute. This intuition of Weil's seems to be compatible with some recent insights of contemporary theological reflection, which provide certainly more nuanced developments of the theme of Christ as 'mediator'. The theologian Piero Coda, for example, states that, 'Through his death on the cross, which completes the "self-dispossession" through love,[9] starting with the incarnation and leading to the total gift of himself, Christ discloses his mediation to the Father as a direct and filial relationship among persons and with him. He does this by means of his descent into the abyss of the human condition, and also by the distancing he experienced from God, through which he includes us in himself and identifies us with himself, identifying himself with us by particularizing his universal reality as Word of God made flesh.'[10]

Weil sees the redemption worked by Christ as the one event that prolongs his coming both backwards and forwards in time, giving meaning to history and accounts of the past. Even if they anticipated Christ in actuality, there can have been certain 'redeeming' figures who, in imitation of him, have been 'mediators': these are pure beings capable of redeeming the world itself in their own manner, through being capable of 'mediation' – and 'all mediation', Weil writes. 'is God'.[11] In the same way, also, 'through those who before and after [his] birth have imitated Christ', the world has been able to recover meaning, simply and solely on account of their 'rootedeness' in their own religion and thanks to the mediators this has produced.

As Tommasi rightly observes, 'Simone Weil holds that it is not possible to reach God except through the narrow gate assigned to us: for us, for the West that was Christian and is now completely de-Christianized, the way to the sacred and to a possible rehabilitation is only that indicated in the Gospels'. Emphasizing the 'rootedness' in one's own tradition does not, in Weil's view,

mean denying the centrality of Christ; on the contrary, it means spreading it
to infinity. For her, Christ is the 'model' for all mediators and all mediation,
and the model that, through becoming incarnate, redeems those who have
gone before him as well those who have come after him.

Upholding this 'rootedness' is a splendid stratagem through which Weil
succeeds in saving both the centrality of Christ and the oneness of different faiths (one's own religion and 'all religions', she says, 'are the only true
ones') as well as ecumenical and inter-religious openness to other revelations.[12] Weil's ontology, according to Coda, 'revealed in her use of prejudice-
free religious language in its pluriform universal expression, together with
her decided christological singularity [is] an ontology – as E. Gabellieri has
shown – of freedom and gift.[13] Following this route (to return to Coda),

> [W]e manage to discern and define [. . .] the discriminating hermeneuti-
> cal key that inspires and regulates Weil's entire symbolic discourse: this is
> the key she finds in Jesus Christ not as one symbol among many but as the
> 'true metaphor' in which symbolic language expressing the asymmetrical
> relationship between human longings and God's gift of grace ultimately
> justifies itself, becoming the setting for the mediation-in-the-act between
> eternity and time, in the 'once and for all' unique historical event of
> Christ's pasch, which happens ever-anew in the holy Spirit making itself
> present to the free choice that appropriates it, and in doing so becomes
> what it – sometimes only confusedly – perceives itself called to become.[14]
> [. . .] As a precursor, in effect, of those Vatican II orientations taken up and
> re-launched in the prophetic – in words and deeds[15] – teaching of John
> Paul II, Weil forces herself (as she writes in *Letter to a Religious*) into a
> basic re-thinking of the very notion of faith: the fact that people can attain
> salvation outside the visible confines of the Church,[16] and that 'salvation
> does not come about without a "new birth", without inner enlightenment,
> without the presence of Christ and the Holy Spirit in the soul.'[17] Weil's
> work [. . .] provides valuable encouragement to travel in this direction, in
> the strictest faithfulness to that Light 'which enlightens everyone' (John
> 1.9) and which became flesh (cf. John 1.14) in Jesus the Christ.

Translated by Paul Burns

Notes

1. 'Person and Impersonal in Simone Weil' was the central topic of the convention held at the 'Personalist Research Centre' at Teramo in Italy from 10 to 12 December 2008 – *trans.*

2. Simone Weil's complete works are published in French: *Oeuvres complètes*, Paris: Gallimard, 1989–94. English translations from various publishers. See *The Notebooks of Simone Weil*, London: Routledge, 1984 (here from Ital. trans. *Quaderni IV*, 1993, p. 113).

3. *Quaderni IV*, p. 382.

4. As exemplified by the humanists Pico della Mirandola and Nicholas of Cusa.

5. W. Tommasi, *Simone Weil: segni, idoli e simboli*, Milan: Franco Angeli, 1993, p. 209.

6. *Quaderni III*, p. 415.

7. *Ibid.*

8. *Ibid.*, p. 49.

9. Cf. Phil. 2.7.

10. P. Coda, *Il logos e il nulla. Trinità, religioni, mistica*, Rome: Città Nuova, 2003, pp. 468–9.

11. *Ibid.*, p. 415.

12. Weil continually stresses the fact that all mystics express their relationship with the divine using the language of their own tradition: the relationship with God always takes the 'I–thou' form, a dialogue that is possible only on the basis of the language and traditions within which one lives.

13. Cf. E. Gaballiere, *Être et don. Simone Weil et la philosophie*, Louvain and Paris: Peeters, 2003.

14. P. Coda, Preface to M. Marianelli, *La Metafora ritrovata. Miti e simboli nella filosofia di Simone Weil*, Rome: Città Nuova, 2004.

15. I am thinking of the World Day of Prayer by the religions for peace, held at the Pope's behest in Assisi in 1986.

16. Cf. LG 16; GS 21; AG 7.

17. S. Weil, *Lettre à un religieux*, 1951, here Ital. trans. p. 48.

President Lugo: A Dream Frustrated?

MARGOT BREMER

The extraordinary historic moment we are experiencing in Paraguay is generating two opposed tendencies: one is the quest for new paradigms, and the other is the reaction against this – rejecting change and clinging to old ways. Setting out to seek alternatives in the midst of epochal change seems easy, because the need is plain to see. Nevertheless, it is by no means easy to put oneself forward as an alternative in the middle of a current of meddlesome people seeking to assure their own security out of fear of future uncertainty. This is the situation of Paraguay under its president Fernando Lugo, former bishop of San Pedro.

After sixty-one years of (un-)government by the *Colorado* Party, its last president, Nicanor Duarte Frutos summed up in his person the greed for power and domination that characterized the party.[1] At the end of his term, having failed in his attempt to be re-elected, he prepared to become a senator, campaign chief, and party leader. As his candidate for the presidency, he chose a woman, his education minister Blanca Ovelar, a distant relative of his. But Blanca failed to 'take', and this was one of many reasons why the *Colorados* finally lost power.

Our citizenry had already taken cognizance of the alternative scenario, dating from the first World Social Forum held in Porto Alegre in 2003 and proclaimed through the next eight Fora: 'Another world is possible'. With a third of the population living in extreme poverty, the motto of a society in which there was room for all became the goal and inspiration for many Paraguayans. It soon became clear that if there was to be a real change, it was not enough to go to polling booths and cast one's vote, but there had to be a change of mentality, a deconstruction of the old ways and incrusted structures of the 'perennial' party, replacing them with another, more democratic order.

The people had the right to hope, hope that had been denied them for years with the argument that 'this is just how things are'. It seemed impossible to be able to change the party in power: being *Colorado* and voting for the party was what it meant to be Paraguayan.[2] Voting for a non-*colorado* party was seen as treachery to the country; this was the only party for government. But despite growing expectations of a change it seemed that no one would dare to change parties when the time came to vote. Until, that is, a totally unexpected and unforeseeable candidate appeared, one who seemed to have the qualities to bring about change: Fernando Lugo, former bishop of San Pedro, the poorest Department in the whole of Paraguay.

I. The surprise of Lugo's victory

The day came when the Paraguayan people showed through the ballot box that they were tired of the traditional corrupt system. They broke decisively from it, changing the paradigm of the presidential figure. Nothing could persuade the people not to vote for Lugo: not the TV or radio campaigns and the money poured into them, nor the free roasts and mobile phones, nor the free medicines (stolen from the Institute for Social Welfare), nor the episcopal warnings that Lugo was not eligible, nor the *colorado* (red) blouses and scarves, nor the collection boxes for the dead poor of the *Colorado* faction, nor all their strategies, proven over sixty years. The people were disillusioned and tired; they opted for Lugo, someone who was close to them, a simple man, religious in the true sense, alternative. Not even he could believe his electoral victory; far less could the *Colorados* believe and accept their defeat.

One of the first things said by the new Forty-seventh President of Paraguay was: 'We shall build democracy together', words spoken on 20 April 2008 near the square where nine years earlier the famous 'Paraguay March' came about, in which eight youngsters lost their lives defending the democratic process just begun. On the blood of these martyrs for their country, Lugo planned to build, together with the citizens of Paraguay, *our* Paraguayan democracy.

It should be stressed that Lugo won the election not only because the people had grown tired of the *Colorado* Party over the course of six decades; it was also the person of the fresh candidate that held attraction and promise: his personal charisma, his social commitment, his theological line (liberation theology), his honesty and simplicity, his struggles during his time as bishop and before that – since he was a theology student – alongside social movements, his openness to all sectors of society, since he belonged to no political party. However, a Christian Democrat by inclination and used to administering a diocese, Lugo had no other experience in the field of public administration – and neither did those he chose to form the new ministerial team. Furthermore, he had to be prepared to 'live with the enemy', since the *Colorados* held on to the majority in Parliament, the same intransigent lot that could still not swallow their defeat. In effect, his margin for taking action was not very wide if he was to begin making changes.

After so many years of political disaster, the expectations aroused were immense and enormously varied. But it is well known that real changes start at home. We cannot be externally other than we are internally. The people lacked this vision of changing themselves; they were used to expecting everything to arrive from the top down, from any new regime with its *caudillo* of the people, or *tendotá*, as we say here. Bringing about a new understanding that change could only truly come about if we *all*, or at least the majority, change presented the new president with a great challenge. Furthermore, after sixty years of un-government, the people are impatient; they want to see rapid and visible change, without realizing that it is a slow, organic, and organized process.

II. First symbolic steps to change

Lugo was reduced to the lay state by Pope Benedict XVI. This does not mean that he renounced his belonging to the Church. As brand-new president of Paraguay, and conscious of the lay basis of his Christian Baptism, he said in his inaugural speech on 15 August 2008 that, 'This layman, eternally grateful to his Mother Church, will remain firm in the solidarity of his faith to the end of his humble history'. Leonardo Boff, a close friend of Fernando Lugo, linked through their liberation theology, declared as a guest at the ceremony that his friend, 'seeks to exercise power giving the central place to the poor and the Guaraní people. He has made it clear that he does not want to make politics his destiny in life but only to pass by rendering a service.'

Another symbol of change is the sandals Lugo has worn every day since then. He gave another clear sign the following month by abolishing once and for all the pomp and display of power, which helped to emphasize the lavish expenditure of the rich in the face of the needs of the poor. Lugo began 'the exercise of power under the principle of austerity'.[3]

In his inaugural address, Lugo encouraged dreams of a new Paraguay with deep roots: 'the dream of a future with Paraguayan identity'. To achieve this, he promised to search the past and 'find its values and signs so that the semiotic of the future can find clear motivations that call for a tomorrow that repeats the successes and avoids the errors'. He recovered a value that runs very deep in all the indigenous cultures of this land, adopted by the Paraguayans: inclusion, the complete opposite of neo-liberalism, which champions exclusion. He bravely and courageously declared: 'We want a Paraguay in which *all* may grow'. He summarized the historical course from Independence in 1811, reclaiming the utopia of the great leader José Gaspar Rodríguez de Francia, his personal ideal of a president. He invited his audience to recall that lost dream and to re-build it 'on the virtues of solidarity, social equality, and the identity we share'. He also appealed to the memory of the López, to 'bring back the worthiness of governments whose combination of honesty and austerity equated to the supreme sacrifice for the country'. He appealed to the *kairotic* present moment, at which it is possible to build a new Paraguay, if all contribute their share: 'Now is the time to look to the future and intrepidly apply the collective engineering of the future of Paraguay, without belittling effort, without falling on the path, without lowering the dreams . . . of hope, but cultivating the seed of a new Paraguay project'. It seemed that Lugo was seeking to inaugurate the possibility of a new history based on the Guaraní matrix of the 'Search for the Land without Evil', the main influence on Paraguayan culture, but which has never managed to infiltrate its politics.

III. First difficulties

Fernando Lugo's actions as president-elect had aroused a degree of interest among the people seldom seen before. At first people could see that the steps taken by his government-elect were measured by expectations of change and changes of direction toward correcting the abuses of power we had experienced over the nineteen years of transition to democracy, from 1989 to 2008.

A small sign of change was two close relatives of Lugo withdrawing from the public positions they had allowed themselves to be nominated for. But this is not enough: Lugo's credibility will be measured by his ability to change the situation of the country, especially at the level of justice and equity of distribution of wealth, defence of the natural heritage, and food production.

The people of Paraguay are gradually coming to see that without the support of the citizens, Fernando Lugo is little or nothing. He has been a figure in whom citizens can trust: he is a man of the Church; he is not corrupt; he does not have the history of politicking and power-seeking that his predecessors had. Unsurprisingly, though, he has had to face up to numerous difficulties, especially from the oligarchy, which does not seek the same alternatives.

The first has been the appointment of ministers, in which Lugo had his hands tied through not having his own party. The more important ones – Finance, Public Works, Agriculture and Livestock, Industry and Commerce, Interior, Education, Health, Chancellery – ended up (with the exceptions of Finance, Interior, and Health) in the hands of more conservative sectors, though more progressive individuals, whom Lugo could trust absolutely, occupied the lesser ministries – Social Services, Women, Culture, Children, Young People. This spread caused a considerable drop in expectation of real change, though all will depend on how Lugo handles the situation.

The second lies in the fact that the press and communications media are virtually all controlled by enemies of the new government, which has raised innumerable obstacles to bringing about the desired change. In the pay of the opposition, they distort the news, emphasize superficialities, mock the president's little errors, bring prejudice into official announcements, always against Lugo, never in his favour.[4] So the new administration is always under attack from the mass media.

Finally, Lugo has no party to support him. Lacking his own, he won the election with the support of the 'Patriotic Alliance for Change' (APC), made up of the traditional opposition party, the 'Authentic Radical Liberal Party' (PLRA), together with the *Oviedistas* (supporters of Lino Oviedo), a wing of the *Colorados*, and other small opposition parties and social movements. In Paraguay, however, building alliances implies ceding quotas of power, and we know too that memory does not play a major role in the Paraguayan consciousness. The young sociologist Diego Segovia predicts: 'The risk . . . is that the energy generated by the healthy returns from the ballot boxes [on 20 April 2008] will not outlast the ephemeral nature of the euphoria unleashed. If this happens, everything will go back to normal, since a change of orchestral conductor does not cure the intellectual and moral ineptitude of its members.'[5] The only support Lugo can count on is that of the social movements and the generality of the population.

IV. A painful Easter

In Holy Week this year the news that Lugo had fathered a child broke like a bombshell. The following Monday he reacted publicly, acknowledging his son. Those of us who trusted in him as a man of integrity, unlike all the country's previous politicians, did not find it easy to accept this news. In a different way, we experienced another 'painful Easter'.[6] A group of young Jesuits expressed their disillusion in a public letter, declaring: 'Faced with the admission of his paternity and the subsequent accusations, disappointment and mistrust began to set in, leading to indignation and shame; we found ourselves in a growing cloud of questions concerning the president's ability to remain consistent with the words to which he is committed. . . . On the social and national level it seemed that the whole journey made and the dreams of transforming the country had come tumbling down.' The event unleashed an international storm of scandalized publications, since such a thing was not expected of a man of the Church, a bishop and a Religious vowed to celibacy. The Catholic Church was the sector that suffered most damage. The people, however, reacted in a different way. They already knew similar things of so many other priests, monks, nuns, and even bishops that they saw it as a simple weakness, in no way comparable to the abuses of previous presidents.

The press and mass media found this scandal the best hook with which publicly to pull down Lugo's moral authority. Irreverently, jokingly, cynically, and woundingly, they blew up this incident in Lugo's private life. Despite this, the paparazzi discovered, in a poll they carried out soon after the revelation, that Lugo's popularity had not fallen nearly as much as they expected. But the press has found a further ongoing argument for chasing Lugo's mistakes and dedicating itself to propagating them as the only truth about him. Since Easter 2009 the mass media have not stopped bombarding Lugo with unfounded suspicions and accusations of other children, but they have done so in an infuriating, infantile, and polemical manner, behaving without any hint that there might be a higher school of journalism. They look for the mote in his eye without seeing the beam in the eyes of those who are paying them to act like this.

Thanks be to God, the effect has been quite the opposite of what they sought to provoke: the people, respectful and better-mannered, have been disgusted by their language and have deepened and renewed their option for Lugo, with growing commitment day by day. Lugo himself has gradually grown in strength in the midst of this 'storm'; he has not given up on his project. And this has convinced the Paraguayan people to forgive him for all the 'putting his foot in it' that the press try to present to the people as evidence of their president's political incompetence. The Paraguayan people, who are deeply religious, respect Lugo as a man of faith. The Jesuit students caught this experience of faith in Fernando Lugo when they wrote: 'Those who are firm in their faith and commitment, though shaken and battered, are not letting themselves be put down'.[7]

V. Resistance to change

The citizenry still keep their trust in their elected president; they do not doubt his rectitude, despite internal conflicts with the vice-president, despite the withdrawal of the PLRA from the Patriotic Alliance for Change, despite all the minor contretemps. Lugo still remains close to the people and is sticking to his good intentions – even if on the diplomatic level he still puts his foot in it through lack of political experience: he is on a learning curve.

In the midst of the financial crisis and the concentration of conservative forces in the country, Lugo is keeping to the course of change. The impresario and publicist Pascual Rubiani has commented prophetically: 'Being able to direct a recession scenario successfully will perhaps prove the greatest challenge facing Lugo's government. . . . The steering process necessary to ensure a peaceful and ordered change in institutions will, undoubtedly, put our president's capacity for political negotiation to the test.'[8] After the electoral change, now the political change has to come. But in all this let us not forget that this change cannot come from Lugo alone but is in the hands of the whole population.

Every day the oligarchy show increasing signs of resistance to change. The global financial crisis, on a level not experienced since the 'black Friday' of 1929, is making the moneyed minority fearful of losing their wealth. This is impelling them to take a hard right-wing line. They accuse Lugo of aligning himself preferentially with left-wing Latin American presidents. Because he embodies a progressive stance, he is seen by his enemies as left-wing – and not only by his enemies, on account of his option for the poor, which poses a great threat to them. They ask whether Lugo is going to carry out a fresh redistribution of wealth on socialist lines, whether he will enact laws or make political decisions that will limit the illicit gains they were used to from the *Colorado* era, when total immunity was guaranteed. Others, in the financial and business sectors, as well as civil servants and professionals, are opposed to change for fear that they will no longer be able to buy judges and bypass laws. They are the ones who objected to the introduction of a wealth tax, the fairest form of taxation. For the same reason they do not want to see the Supreme Court made independent, since it now works in their favour.

Behind this resistance to change there obviously lie group and individual interests that see Lugo as an enemy determined to pull down their 'castles' for the sake of greater social equality. In order to disguise this petty-minded attitude, they accuse Lugo of doing nothing, of being ineffective, making themselves look like the political movers. Their criticism is bitter, harsh, and destructive, with no constructive element to it, showing that they have no intention of collaborating in the building of a new Paraguay.

I want to reiterate here Lugo's insistence that change, meaning the building of a new democracy, has to be made by everyone. Lugo on his own, without the people, can do nothing. This implies a necessary change in the mindset of all citizens of Paraguay, in order to deconstruct the paradigms introjected by previous administrations and to reconstruct new political paradigms. Furthermore, for any political and social change to come about, people need to be clear about what they want to change and to use this input to measure the effects of change on the people. We also know that significant structural changes necessarily have to be accompanied by changes in the behaviour of a whole nation that has had political models of non-government, laziness, corruption, and deceit, leading down the decades to repercussions on the conduct and survival of the people. This Paraguayan people needs – besides its dream of democracy – education if it is to collaborate in building it, since it has never known a democracy in its history. In this sense, it has no model on which to call. This means an alternative system of education, with active participation in popular organizations in order to fight against the established and even sanctioned corruption and impunity, since 'in the dark, without witnesses, all are corrupted' (José Nicolás Morínigo). The people also need to learn how to discuss possible changes without confronting the immovable positions that generally characterize televised parliamentary debates. All this remains work in progress for Lugo together with the people to be able to build the dreamed-of democracy. Despite all the resistance, I believe the changes can be made. So I want to balance the real threat to change with these heartening words by Juan Manuel Fadul, brother of the founder of the 'Beloved Nation' Party: 'Lugo's base and support is indestructible. . . . It is not his morality or his credibility but much more than these: his great love for life and for the poorest!'[9]

Conclusion

This short survey of Lugo's unusual course shows that we cannot speak of Lugo, as president of the Republic of Paraguay, alone. Lugo has joined his life to the destiny of his people. Speaking of Lugo means speaking of the Paraguayan people and of change. And this is perhaps his most challenging and most democratic achievement: the people feel summoned to collaborate in building the first real democracy their country has known. Now that they realize this, the process of change has already begun.

The people of Paraguay are not looking for their president to be a new Messiah, nor the traditional sort of leader: they are looking him to be the man Fernando, who together with them has taken on the commitment to change this country. For those who elected him, he is 'the first opportunity in their lives to build a new nation'.[10] Lugo is not yet a dream frustrated, and the people of Paraguay still place their trust in him.

Translated by Paul Burns

Notes

1. The *Colorado* Party is that of the dictator Stroessner; it managed to adapt in accordance with democratic laws, without being capable of recycling itself and changing its dominant mentality into a democratic one.
2. More than 50% of the population was formerly *Colorado*; that scenario has now shifted substantially.
3. S. Ruffrinelli, Editorial, *Acción* 287 (Sept. 2008), 4.
4. For example, the radio announces, 'Listen to this lie by the new minister of education . . .'; or a photo of Lugo on a Kawasaki 800 motorbike, in the most widely read daily in Paraguay, is captioned, 'Lugo shows the journalists his new toy' (ABC Color, 4 Apr. 2009), p. 26.
5. D. Segovia, 'Aires nuevos y desfíos grandes', *Acción* 284 (June 2008), 26.
6. Expression applied to the Paraguayan 'Christian Agrarian Leagues', formed in the 1970s and dedicated to living the gospel in radical fashion. The agricultural workers were accompanied by a group of Religious, mainly Jesuit and Franciscan priests, who were persecuted by the Stroessner regime and expelled from the country. Many committed league members were arrested and tortured, and several were put to death at Easter 1973. The only book on this unique movement is David Hernández, *La herejía de seguir a Jesús. Intrahistoria de las Ligas Agrarias Cristianas del Paraguay*, Madrid: IEPALA Ed., 2003.
7. Jesuit students of the Ignacio Ellacuría Community, Barrio Trinidad, Asunción, 'Aportes y Reflexiones sobre las denuncias contra Lugo', 28 Apr. 2009, p. 2.
8. P. Rubiani, 'Los desafíos del cambio en Paraguay, Coyuntura política', *Acción* 291 (Feb. 2009), 9.
9. *Ibid.*
10. *Ibid.*, 3.

Contributors

PIERRE GIBERT is a Jesuit priest, born in 1936. He holds a degree in literature and human sciences from the Sorbonne in Paris. A Doctor of Theology, he is an Old Testament exegete. He holds an honorary professorship at the Catholic University of Lyon. From 1998 to 2008 he was editor-in-chief of the review *Recherches de Science Religieuse* (RSR). He has published a critical edition of the *Histoire critique du Vieux Testament* (1678) by Richard Simon (2008); his latest work, *L'invention critique de la Bible. XVe-XVIIIe siècle*, a history of biblical exegesis, is due to be published by Gallimard in late 2009.

Address: 15 rue Monsieur, FN 75007 Paris, France

MARIE-THERES WACKER is Professor of Old Testament and Women's Studies in Theology in the faculty of Catholic Theology of Münster University, Germany. In recent years she has concentrated her research on topics related to biblical monotheism and Hellenistic Judaism and gender issues in the monotheistic religions. In 2005 her institute held the first German-language symposium on approaches to Theological Masculinity Studies (the proceedings were published as *Mannsbilder. Kritische Männerforschung und theologische Frauenforschung im Gespräch* (ed. Marie-Theres Wacker and Stefanie Rieger-Goertz, 2006).

Address: Katholisch-TheologischeFakultät, Seminar für Exegese des Alten Testaments, Johannisstraße 8-10, Sekretariat Raum 2.14, 48143 Münster, Germany
E-mail: wacker.mth@uni-muenster.de

JOSÉ LUIS SÁNCHEZ NOGALES, a Catholic priest of the diocese of Almería (Spain), is Professor of Philosophy of Religion at the faculty of theology at Granada University. He has recently been nominated Director of the 'Andalusia Chair for Religious Dialogue'. His sixteen books on philosophy and religion include the widely-known *Filosofía y Fenomenología de la Religión* (2003), and he has also published sixteen contributions to collective works and 62 articles in several reviews. Dr Sánchez Nogales has directed five courses that took place in Granada under the general title 'Christians and Muslims'. He participates frequently in congresses and study journeys, especially in Europe and North Africa. He recently gave several lectures in Frankfurt, Bordeaux, and Amman on Christian-Islamic dialogue in Spain, the subject of his most recent book, *El Islam en la España actual* (2008). Since 2005 he has been an adviser to the Commission for Religious Relations with Muslims established by the Pontifical Council for Inter-religious Dialogue.

Address: Facultad de Teología de Granada, Campus Universitario Cartuja, Apdo. Postal 2002, 18080 – Granada (Spain).
E-mail: nogales@teol-granada.com

CATHERINE CORNILLE is Associate Professor of Comparative Theology at Boston College and has also taught at the University of Leuven in Belgium. Her research interests focus on theoretical and methodological questions in the study of religions and inter-religious dialogue, as well on the relationship between religion and culture in the contemporary context of globalization. She has published widely on the phenomenon of new religious movements, inculturation, and inter-religious dialogue. Her most recent book is entitled *The Im-Possibility of Interreligious Dialogue* (2008). She is also editor of *Many Mansions: Multiple Religious Belonging and Christian Identity* (2002) and of *Song Divine: Christian Commentaries on the Bhagavadgita* (2006). She is managing editor of the series 'Christian Commentaries on non-Christian Sacred Texts'.

Address: 141 Endean Drive, Walpole, MA 02032, USA

MARIA CLARA LUCCHETTI BINGEMER is a lecturer and researcher in the theology department of the Pontifical Catholic University of Rio de Janeiro (PUC-RJ). She gained a doctorate in systematic theology from the Gregorian in Rome, with a thesis on trinitarian mysticism and Christian praxis in St Ignatius of Loyola. She is currently Dean of the theology centre and the human sciences faculty of the PUC-RJ. For ten years she directed the Centro Loyola de Fé e Cultura, which aims to offer lay people in particular an integral (human, spiritual, doctrinal and ethical) formation by means of dialogue between faith, culture, and other religious traditions. Her most recent works are *Deus*

Trindade, a Vida no Coração do Mundo (with Vitor Feller, 2008); *A argila e o espírito* (articles and essays; 2004); *Um rosto para Deus?* (2005); *Simone Weil – A força e a fraqueza do amor* (2007).

Address: Pontifícia Universidade Católica do Rio de Janeiro, Depto. de Teologia (TEO), Rua Marquês de São Vicente, 225, Edifício Cardeal Leme 11 andar, Caixa Postal: 38097, 22453-900 - Rio de Janeiro - RJ – Brasil
E-mail: agape@puc-rio.br

ANDRÉS TORRES QUEIRUGA was born in 1940 and holds doctorates in philosophy from the University of Santiago de Compostela and in theology from the Gregorian in Rome. He taught fundamental theology at the Theological Institute in Santiago from 1968 to 1987 and is currently professor of philosophy of religion at the university there. He is editor of *Encrucillada: Revista Galega de Pensamento Cristián*, as well as being on the editorial board of *Iglesia Viva*, an advisor to *Revista Portuguesa de Filosofia*, and a founding member of the Spanish Society for Sciences of Religion. His many published works include *Constitución y evolución del dogma* (1977); *Recuperar la salvación* (1977, ³2001); *Creo en Dios Padre* (⁵1998); *Recuperar la creación* (1997; German trans. 2008); *Fin del cristianismo premoderno* (2000); *Repensar la resurrección* (2003); *Esperanza a pesar del mal* (2005); *Repensar la revelación (*2008; revised ed. of 1977, trans. into Italian, Portuguese and German).

Address: O. Courraliña 23 G, 15705 Santiago de Compostela, La Coruña, Spain
E-mail: atorres@usc.es/ torresqueiruga@gmail.com

ERICO HAMMES is Titular Professor of Systemtic Theology at the Pontifical Catholic University of Rio Grande do Sul, where he researches christology, trintarian theology, and philosophy of religion, as well as peace studies and dialogue with the human sciences. He holds a Doctorate in Theology from the Gregorian Pontifical University in Rome, and his main area of concern is reflecting Latin American tinking in dialogue with recent European theology, especially that of Bonhoeffer, Moltmann, and Rahner.

Address: FATEO – PUCRS, Av. Ipiranga, 6681, 90619-900 – Porto Alegre (RS), Brazil

LUIZ CARLOS SUSIN is Professor of Systematic Theology at the Pontifical Catholic University of Rio Grande do Sul and at the Higher School of

Theology and Franciscan Spirituality, both in Porto Alegre, Brazil. He is a former President of the Brazilian Society for Theology and Religious Studies, and Secretary General of the World Forum for Theology and Liberation. His recent research has been into the relationship between theology and ecology. His publications include *A Criação de Deus* (2003); *Deus, Pai, Filho e Espirito Santo*; *Jesus, Filho de Deus e Filho de Maria*; *Assim na terra como no céu*, some published by Paulinas (São Paulo) and some by Vozes (Petrópolis).

Address: Rua Juarez Távora, 171, 91520-100 Porto Alegre (RS), Brazil
E-mail: lcsusin@pucrs.br

MICHAEL AMALADOSS, S.J. is the Director of the Institute of Dialogue with Cultures and Religions, Chennai, India. His latest major book is *Beyond Dialogue. Pilgrims to the Absolute*.

Address: Institute of Dialogue with Cultures and Religions, Loyola College, Nungambakkam, Chennai – 600 034, India.

ERIK BORGMAN, born in Amsterdam in 1957, is Professor of Systematic Theology and Theology of Religion, especially Christianity, in the Department of Religious Studies and Theology of Tilburg University, The Netherlands. He is married with two daughters and is a Lay Dominican. Borgman studied philosophy and theology at the University of Nijmegen. He has written a dissertation on the different forms of liberation theology and their relation to academic Western theology (promotion 1990). Between 1998 and 2004 he worked for the Dutch Province of the Order of Preachers to study and keep alive the theology of Edward Schillebeeckx. He has published *Edward Schillebeeckx: a Theologian in his History* (Vol. I: A Catholic Theology of Culture, 2003). Between 2000 and 2007 he worked at the interdisciplinary Heyendaal Institute for theology, sciences, and culture at Radboud University Nijmegen, from 2004 as its academic director. He publishes extensively on the relationship between theology, religion, the Christian tradition, and contemporary culture. He is a member of the Board of Directors and the Presidential Board of Concilium.

Address: Department of Religious Studies and Theology, kamer/Office D 146, PO Box 90153, NL – 5000 LE Tilburg
E-mail: E.P.N.M.Borgman@uvt.nl

PAUL EPPE was born in 1937 in Greven in Germany, the second of six children. He studied business administration at Münster University, where he was awarded a Doctorate in Politics and Economics there in 1972. After a career lasting over thirty years in banking and construction, in 1996 he turned to the study of theology and philosophy at the Catholic Theology faculty of Münster University. In 2008 he was awarded a DD there for his thesis on 'Karl Rahner: between philosophy and theology – departure or demolition?' Paul Eppe is married and has two adult sons.

Address: Droste-zu-Senden-Str. 26, D-48308 Senden, Germany
E-mail: paul.eppe@t-online.de

ROSINO GIBELLINI holds doctorates in theology from the Gregorian University in Rome and in philosophy from the Catholic University of Milan. He is literary director of Editrice Queriniana in Brescia, for which he has founded and directs the collections 'Giornale di teologia' and 'Biblioteca di teologia contemporanea', with the aim of opening Italian theology and culture to international theological thought. He is the author of studies on Teilhard de Chardin, Moltmann, and Pannenberg. His most recent publications include *La teologia del XX secolo* (1992; ⁶2007, enlarged); and he has edited the collective volumes *Dio nella filosofia del Novecento* (1993, ⁶2004) and *Prospettive teologiche per il XXI secolo* (2003, ²2006).

Address: Editrice Queriniana, Via E.Ferri, 75, 25123 Brescia, Italy

MASSIMILIANO MARIANELLI is a lecturer at Perugia University and professor at the Sophia University in Loppiano, Florence. He has recently been working on the thought of Simone Weil, focusing specifically on the subject of myth and publishing *La metafora ritrovata: miti e simboli nella filosofia di Simone Weil* (2004), awarded the 'Medaglia del Pontificato' by the Pontificium Consilium de Cultura in 2005. His other publications include *Alberto Burri l'equilibrio squilibrato: Estetica della rifigurazione* (2005); 'A verdade dos mitos em Simone Weil', in *Simone Weil. Ação e contemplção* (2005); 'Unicité de la vérité et universalisme religieux weilien comme lieu de rencontre entre les cultures', *Cahiers Simone Weil*, XXIX, n° 4 (Dec. 2006), 373–89; 'Los mitos y la fraternidad entre los hombres: Simone Weil y el "lugar" del encuentro', in *El principio olvidado: la fratenidad en la política y el derecho*, ed. A. M.

Baggio (2006), pp. 95–117; *Ontologia della relazione, la convenientia in figure e momenti del pensiero filosofico* (2008).

Address: Via Carlo Marx, 15, 06016 Lama (PG), Italy
E-mail: colbi@inwind.it

MARGOT BREMER was born in Germany and is a Religious of the Sacred Heart of Jesus. She studied pedagogy and theology and holds a Licentiate in Biblical Theology from Granada University in Spain. She has spent 21 years in Paraguay, teaching classes, courses, and workshops. For 17 years she has worked as theological counsellor to the Indigenous Pastoral Council of the Episcopal Conference of Paraguay. She studied Cultural Anthropology on a distance-learning course with the Polytechnic Universities of Ecuador and Munich. She has thrice been a member of the theology team of the Latin American Conference of Religious (CLAR), and since 1989 has collaborated with the Review *Acción*. She now accompanies the indigenous peoples of Paraguay in working out and developing their theological reflection.

Address: C/Tavapy 1825, Barrio Nazareth, Asunción, Paraguay
E-mail: margotbremer@hotmail.com

Concilium Subscription Information

February   2009/1: *Evil Today and Struggles to be Human*

April   2009/2: *Which Religious Heritages for the Future?*

June   2009/3: *Eco-theology*

October   2009/4: *Monotheism – Divinity and Unity Reconsidered*

December   2009/5: *Fathers of the Church in Latin America*

New subscribers: to receive *Concilium 2009* (five issues) anywhere in the world, please copy this form, complete it in block capitals and send it with your payment to the address below.

- -

Please enter my subscription for *Concilium 2009*

Individuals

____ £40.00 UK
____ £60.00 overseas
____ $110.00 North America/Rest of World
____ €99.00 Europe

Institutions

____ £55.00 UK
____ £75.00 overseas
____ $140 North America/Rest of World
____ €125.00 Europe

Postage included – airmail for overseas subscribers

Payment Details:

Payment must accompany all orders and can be made by cheque or credit card
I enclose a cheque for £/$/€ _____ Payable to SCM-Canterbury Press Ltd
Please charge my Visa/MasterCard (Delete as appropriate) for £/$/€ _____
Credit card number _____
Expiry date _____
Signature of cardholder _____
Name on card _____
Telephone _____E-mail _____

Send your order to *Concilium*, SCM-Canterbury Press Ltd
13–17 Long Lane, London EC1A 9PN, UK
E-Mail: office@scm-canterburypress.co.uk

Customer service information:
All orders must be prepaid. Subscriptions are entered on an annual basis (i.e. January to December). No refunds on subscriptions will be made after the first issue of the Journal has been despatched. If you have any queries or require information about other payment methods, please contact our Customer Services department.